IRON-AGE FARM
The Butser Experiment

IRON-AGE FARM

The Butser Experiment

Peter J. Reynolds

A Colonnade Book.

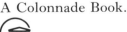

Published by British Museum Publications Limited

Colonnade Books
are published by British Museum Publications Ltd
and are offered as contributions to the enjoyment, study
and understanding of art, archaeology and history.

The same publishers also produce the official
publications of the British Museum.

© 1979 Peter J. Reynolds
ISBN 0 7141 8015 7 paper
ISBN 0 7141 8014 9 cased

Published by British Museum Publications Ltd
6 Bedford Square, London WC1B 3RA

Acknowledgments
The author and publishers are grateful to Mr
J. K. Wycherley for processing and printing
the photographs, and also to the Trustees of the
British Museum for permission to reproduce the
photographs on pages 8 and 10.

Designed by Paul Sharp

Set in Monophoto Imprint and printed and bound in Great Britain by
William Clowes and Sons Limited, Beccles and London

Contents

To My Parents

Preface

The Butser Ancient Farm Research Project was set up primarily to explore theories and ideas suggested by the findings of archaeologists. The results which appear in the text are necessarily interim in nature because they represent part of a process. If they become 'out of date' within ten years the author will be more than content because it will indicate that archaeological thought is developing, theories are under constant review, and new and better techniques are being applied.

The views and theories expressed in this book are those of the author and are not necessarily shared by the members of the Butser Ancient Farm Research Project Committee. At the same time the author acknowledges his great debt to that Committee for their committed support and guidance. Professor W. F. Grimes, Committee Chairman until 1976, and his successor Professor J. Evans of the Institute of Archaeology in London, and the Committee Secretary, Mr H. C. Bowen of the Royal Commission for Historical Monuments, have been particularly untiring in their support, advice and encouragement.

The Butser Ancient Farm Research Project was made possible by generous financial support initially from The Ernest Cook Trust, The Radcliffe Trust, The Pilgrim Trust and currently The Leverhulme Trust. Hampshire County Council has provided the land for the farm and the Demonstration Area as well as considerable grant aid. To all these bodies and other organisations and individuals who have made donations of money and materials to the research the author expresses his deep gratitude. Finally, no list of acknowledgments would be complete without reference to the invaluable contributions made by Mr J. K. Langley, the assistant director, and Mrs P. Perry, the project secretary.

Bronze shield from the Thames at Battersea. First century BC or early first century AD.

8

1 Introduction

The Iron Age, broadly spanning the thousand years before the Romans conquered Britain, is one of the most exciting periods of our past, exciting because we know so much and yet so tantalisingly little. We understand from the few classical references that Britain in the Iron Age was a 'fairy isle' set beyond the edge of the civilised world, a land of mystery and fascination deep in 'Oceanus', the sea that marked the edge of the world. At the same time these references tell us that grain and leather, hunting dogs and slaves were exported to the Continent, a statement which argues social and economic stability, and a multi-layered society with production and service industries. The documentary sources also tell us of the Druids, the scholar-priest class, and that it was common practice for the Celtic scholars of Europe to come to Britain for the finest training available.

The commentaries of the greatest Roman general of all, Julius Caesar, attest to the military skill and expertise of the British during his abortive expeditions of 55 and 54 BC. Indeed, it is from his diaries that the first British personality emerges, Cassivellaunus, Chieftain of the Catuvellauni and commander-in-chief of the British forces. The fact that Caesar was thoroughly outgeneralled and outmanoeuvred in his two expeditions to Britain underlines the great resources and organisation which existed in Britain in the first century BC.

The traditional view of the Celts, the name usually given to the Iron-Age people, is that of the 'noble savage'. Professor Piggott described the Ancient Celts as 'swaggering, belching, touchy chieftains and their equally impossible warrior crew, hands twitching to the sword-hilt at the imagined hint of an insult . . . wiping the greasy moustaches that were a mark of nobility.' This description may well be accurate, but one suspects it only applies to a tiny minority of the population which was specifically maintained by the majority as a warrior élite. Such an élite warrior class may well have acted as a protective layer for the rest of society.

For Celtic Britain the documentary evidence is very slight. Virtually all the written material stems from Roman sources, and one cannot doubt but that the Romans were most skilled propagandists. The vast majority of our evidence of the Celts has been recovered by archaeologists, and this is rarely the evidence of personalities or of events, but the remnants of

Electrum torc from the Snettisham Treasure. First century BC.

everyday life: broken pottery, fragments of bone, foundations of houses, ditches and banks, pits and holes. Because the period in question is deep in the remote past the great bulk of the evidence has long since disappeared virtually without trace.

Some magnificent Celtic objects have been discovered entirely by chance. Beautifully worked and decorated shields have been dredged up from the silt of rivers; hoards of gold torcs have been ripped from the ground by earthmoving machines. Such objects, the work of highly skilled craftsmen, bronzesmiths and blacksmiths, goldsmiths and silversmiths, allow us a remarkable insight into the Celtic period. Technologically the Celts were very skilled. Their art form, as these objects prove, was undeniably sophisticated and advanced. The use of line and form suggest an appreciation far beyond the capacity of a greasy moustachioed braggart. Nor is it entirely convincing to credit the artist with a special status and attribute to him the ability to exercise his imaginative skills in an unappreciative society. An art form invariably reflects the philosophy of a culture. The achievement of Celtic art therefore suggests the need for a reappraisal of the traditional views of Celtic society.

More impressive even than these remarkable objects are the Celtic field monuments which survive to this day. Throughout the British countryside great earthworks dating to this period can be found. The most common variety are great ditches cut around hill tops. The excavated material from the ditches was piled up into great banks, some of which were supported with complex timber revetments. Complicated approaches to the interior of these earthworks are not uncommon, with further ditches and banks called 'horn-works' being constructed to protect the entrance. Commonly these sites are called hill forts, the most famous of which is Maiden Castle in Dorset. Only a few interior areas have been excavated but these invariably provide clear evidence of intensive occupation with remains of houses, roads, storage areas and occasionally so-called temples. Given this intensity of occupation it would be far better to consider these sites as hill towns. Indeed, they may well represent the centres of the vital service industries, the prime factor in the development of urban settlement.

There is little doubt both from the documentary and the field evidence that the basic economy of the Iron Age was agricultural. That the economy flourished is attested by the classical references which describe the export of grain and leather, with the implication that there was a regular and consistent surplus achieved by the Celtic farmers. The archaeological remains of prehistoric fields – the low banks called lynchets which form on the downhill edges – can still be found in many parts of Britain, although with the increasing acreage being taken into arable farming today this evidence is rapidly disappearing. The best examples are to be found in southern England especially on the Downland areas, where sheep farming has been the normal practice for the last two thousand years. The majority of excavations, quite understandably, have been carried out to investigate settlements rather than fields. Many of these would seem to be based upon

Ditches and ramparts at Maiden Castle. (Photo by courtesy of Peter Clayton).

an agricultural economy, although as yet we have no real idea of the significance of the majority of the findings, how the settlements relate to one another, or whether there is a direct relationship at all. The paucity of our knowledge is quite remarkable.

The basic problem lies in the lack of material evidence. With the exception of precious metals, gems and pottery, the vast majority of the material used in the Iron Age was vegetable matter. It is only in the most unusual circumstances that this kind of material actually survives. The most typical instance is waterlogging, but the number of waterlogged sites are despairingly few. Those that have been found, notably Glastonbury and Meare Lake Villages in Somerset, have yielded the most valuable evidence we have in this country. The peat bogs of Denmark and Ireland, where the tannic acid has preserved not only timber, seeds and pollen but also human tissue, have given even greater information. These exceptions, however, simply underline the dearth of material from the 'dry' sites. As excavation techniques have improved, carbonised seeds have become another valuable source of evidence for vegetable matter. One presumes that in the disposal of rubbish in bonfires, part of the fire burned without oxygen and this turned wood and seeds into carbon or charcoal. This process preserves the shape of the material, so that it is possible to identify species of trees and, more importantly, species of seed. While it is most unlikely that a fully representative sample of all the seeds of the plants grown in the Iron Age will ever be obtained, the carbonised remains at least give an indication.

Pollen grains recovered from excavations, particularly pollen from peat deposits, also help greatly in identifying the presence and relative abundance of certain plants. In this case, however, since the pollen is usually distributed by wind and falls as a kind of rain, the weight of the pollen grains themselves and the direction of the seasonal prevailing wind will have a significant bearing in the analysis of any sample.

The cases of carbonised seed and pollen grains have been used to demonstrate the enormous difficulties encountered by the archaeologist in any attempt to explain the remote past. The 'harder' evidence, the holes where posts were once set, ditches and banks, pits and gullies, present difficulties only slightly less complex. An appreciation of these problems leads to a ready understanding of the usual archaeological concentration upon fragments or sherds of pottery. Most excavation reports abound with page after page of illustrations of rim sherds and body sherds, simply because this material has survived and can, therefore, be sorted and categorised, measured and analysed. Pottery, especially broken fragments, is virtually indestructible. One period of prehistory is so slightly known in terms of other material evidence that it is even called the 'Beaker period'. It is a sad reflection on the inadequacy of our knowledge that several hundred years of prehistory are defined simply by the shape of a pot. Pottery can help to date a site within a much shorter timespan. In the Romano–British period it has been possible to isolate a particular decade from pottery fragments.

The normal process followed by an archaeologist after the excavation of a site is fairly straightforward. Armed with all the evidence recovered, it is his job to provide an explanation of what the site may have been, its basic economy and its relationship with other sites in the neighbourhood. Naturally, there is a body of evidence from other sites, some of which may be similar in nature, which can act as a series of reference points. In addition, there are the thoughts and explanations of other archaeologists. Each report tends to rely upon those that have gone before. Patterns of post-holes, once isolated, have been used predictively to explain either missing evidence or evidence hidden beyond the edges of the excavated area. Rarely, however, are two sites exactly alike. In contrast to the modern architectural planners, prehistoric man, at least in detail, retained his individuality. Similarly, even pottery production was local, or at best, regional in type and style. Mass production was a doubtful benefit bestowed by the Romans.

Archaeology, by its very nature, is further fraught with problems. When a site is excavated it is destroyed. There is no opportunity to return and reassess the evidence. The archaeologist is, in a sense, in a better position than the doctor; at least some of the latter's mistakes can be exhumed. The evidence recovered from an excavation, therefore, needs to be recorded impeccably. Theoretically, it should be possible to replace each cubic centimetre of material to its original position. Sadly, this is an ideal and at present beyond our reach, but if it could be achieved, it would be possible in the future to re-examine the evidence in the light of fresh knowledge, in fact, to elevate the subject of archaeology into the ranks of a science. Meanwhile, one is forced to rely upon the interpretation of the archaeologist.

Given all the difficulties which the archaeologist faces, and those already described are by no means exhaustive, it is easy to understand a reluctance to accept a straight explanation of an excavation without detailed information. Indeed, even with the detail it would be unwise to accept any explanation uncritically. If archaeology is to become a science, then its findings should be subjected to normal scientific testing. Our scientific knowledge is but an approximation to the truth at any level. Einstein demonstrated this fact with his elegant theory of relativity. How much more removed from the truth, therefore, is archaeological interpretation.

There is a clear case to be made for the empirical testing of archaeological theories and explanations. Necessarily, this does not include the broad generalisations which are based on a large sample of excavations. Rather it is to test the detailed theories upon which the generalisations are founded. In effect, it seeks to discover the 'how' and 'why' of the 'what'. The following chapters of this book present a number of such tests and their results. Throughout there is a concentration upon the material evidence, the post-holes and pits and pottery sherds. It is by studying these objects, how they work and inter-relate that we can get closer to the people.

There is here no thought of playing at being Iron-Age people. Any attempt to relive the remote past is destined to failure, because the knowledge and experience of previous generations are denied us. To place modern man into a prehistoric context, given the limitations of our knowledge, is only to observe how modern people may react both to the conditions and to each other.

The philosophy of the experimental approach is quite different. The material evidence recovered by excavation is the basis for the formulation of an hypothesis. The use of the term 'hypothesis' is preferred to 'interpretation', because the former allows for a margin of error, while the latter suggests accuracy and real knowledge. The next stage is to test the hypothesis for validity by building an experiment. This can be done to test both structures and processes. The experiment should be repeated several times to make sure the results are consistent. Inconsistency of result will suggest that the experiment is in error. On completion, the results, such as a standing structure or the marks left by a process like smelting metal, are compared to the excavated evidence. If there is agreement the hypothesis may be tentatively accepted as valid. If there is no agreement the hypothesis is clearly wrong, and a further hypothesis should be formulated. Occasionally, the experiment will suggest an alternative, for often the side-effects of an experiment provide new information to help

The pit clamp during firing. Turves and loose earth have covered over the fire. It takes about twenty hours for the firing to be completed.

Occasionally the fire burns through the roof cover revealing the fired pots. When this happens the exposed portions of the pots are fired pink and red. The covered pots are reduced or fired black. Temperatures of over 900°C have been achieved in this type of kiln.

answer problems recognised but unsolved in excavations. The
best example is the pit created when firing pottery in a clamp
or contained fire. The intense heat of the firing actually burns
away the underlying chalk rock. After several firings a pit is
created which has clear parallels in archaeological records. In
this case the side-effect offers a valid theory for a particular
feature.

As far as is possible, the individual element of skill is
removed from any experiment. This does not detract from the
experimental process at all, but it does emphasise the danger
of assuming that because an experiment has a valid result it is

therefore right. It also removes the equal danger of assessing the time taken to achieve an end product. An experimenter may take ten hours to accomplish a valid end product which an expert could have achieved in one hour. The transfer of the former result could err by a factor of ten. On the other hand, the modern expert may well be more or even less accomplished than his prehistoric counterpart, and further error may be compounded. Besides, the time element is of less importance initially. First we need to know how and why.

It is important to realise that more than one valid hypothesis can be raised on exactly the same basic data. Therefore, when using hypotheses to explain an excavation, it is necessary to select the one most likely to relate to the whole of the material.

Experiments in archaeology have been carried out from the very beginning of man's interest in his own past. Scientific experiment, on the other hand, is relatively recent and represents the most progressive element in archaeology today. The subject is multi-disciplinary and ranges from thermodynamics through to mycology, the study of fungi and bacteria. Throughout, the standards of each individual science involved are to be adopted. There is a clearly defined gulf between real experiment and demonstration. Both have their place in archaeology, the latter most importantly in explaining comprehensibly to as large an audience as possible the findings of excavation.

One further aid in the explanation of archaeological evidence from prehistory is known generally as comparative ethnology. In certain parts of the world at present there are societies which are regarded as being of prehistoric type. Much has been made of the hunter-gatherer societies and similar residual societies by the cultural anthropologists, and attempts are regularly made to transfer such social organisations into a prehistoric context. In terms of model building this is both instructive and entertaining but with regard to the formula outlined above there is, unfortunately, no possibility of reaching a statement of validity or otherwise. From the experimenter's point of view, certainly for the Iron-Age period here and on the continent, the valuable element is the study of those processes practised by the Iron-Age type societies which leave comparable archaeological data to those already recovered. For example, it is of vital importance to study and record in great detail the way peasant farmers plough with an ard and cattle, since the marks left by this activity can be compared directly with the excavated ard marks of prehistory. In addition, since there is a particular relationship between ploughman and trained cattle, it is also worth studying the treatment and animal husbandry involved. I have long been confused, for example, by some of the Bronze-Age rock carvings from Scandinavia which show a man holding a leafy twig walking in front of the oxen pulling an ard. The ploughman in turn holds a stick which is usually interpreted as a goad. Recently in Spain I saw exactly this scene. The man in front with the leafy twig simply brushed away the flies from the faces of the cattle while the ploughman's 'goad' was used, not to poke cattle, but to free the earth from the point of the ard at each headland. Once observed the process is simple, functional and devoid of ritual. One final *caveat* to be observed in connection with comparative ethnology, and its potential contribution to our understanding of the Iron Age, is that examples must be drawn only from comparable temperate zones. Climatic variation regularly leads to fundamentally different practices.

It was in response to the need for scientific experiment in prehistoric archaeology that the Butser Ancient Farm Research Project was set up in 1972. Its object is to reconstruct a farm dating to about 300 BC, in the mainstream of the Iron Age period. In reality it is an open-air scientific research laboratory, unique in world archaeology. The purpose is to explore all the aspects of such a farm, the structures and processes, the plant cultivation and animal husbandry, and to consider not only how each particular aspect itself may operate but also how all the aspects integrate together. It is a massive and most exciting undertaking. The concept of setting up such a research project goes far beyond a simple reconstruction. It sets out to define the basic evidence, to evaluate and test ideas and theories, and to focus attention upon the essential details. In effect, it adds a new dimension to prehistoric archaeology.

Hay was a vitally important fodder for livestock in the Iron Age, as in succeeding periods. Evidence for haystacks is extremely rare. Other haystacks have been built based upon a solitary post-hole.

2 *The Ancient Farm*

The Ancient Farm is situated on a northern spur of Butser Hill, known locally as Little Butser, approximately three miles south of Petersfield in Hampshire. The area of about fourteen hectares was generously leased at a nominal rent by the County Council to the Ancient Agriculture Committee. It comprises the whole spur including the wooded slopes.

Butser Hill, 271 m above sea level, is the highest down in Hampshire and is physically and archaeologically most impressive. It is like a massive prehistory handbook with a large number of sites from all periods. Geologically, the mass of the hill is middle chalk with a capping of clay with flints. Shaped like the back of the human hand, it has a main plateau area with a number of spurs radiating from it with deep and precipitous valleys between the spurs. In the past it represented a considerable barrier to transport, and up to the late eighteenth century north–south traffic travelled along tracks established in prehistory. The main London-to-Portsmouth road on the eastern flank of the hill has been literally carved out of the living rock in order to provide a less troublesome route. The only easy approach to the top of the hill is from the south-west along gently sloping ground.

From the top of Butser extensive views can be seen in any direction, southwards to the Isle of Wight and the coast, northwards across the Meon and Rother valleys and to the east and west along the line of the South Downs. Before the site was acquired by the County Council in 1966 as an area of outstanding natural beauty, it was farmed intensively. The plateau area was particularly prized as good arable ground for wheat production, while the slopes of the hill were extensively used for sheep grazing. Today the majority of the hill is down to grass and used only for grazing.

The area was exploited in all periods of prehistory and many mesolithic and neolithic flint tools and axes have been found. Scattered over the plateau area on top of the hill are a large number of Bronze-Age barrows and on the southern and eastern flanks there is an extensive 'Celtic' field system, shown by lynchets or low banks which once divided the fields. Each of the spurs which radiate from the hill is cut off from the plateau area by ditches and banks of the Iron-Age period. Initially, it was thought that the hill top might have been intended to become a hill fort or town, but from the nature of the crossdykes this is most unlikely, since they cut across the spur with no attempt to follow round the contours of the hill.

On the south-eastern approach there are two sets of these crossdykes and banks.

So far only two settlement sites have been identified, one of Bronze-Age date a little to the south of Butser Hill, the other of late Bronze Age through the Iron Age on the Little Butser spur itself. The former site, the presence of which was totally unknown, was discovered by chance during engineering works on the London-to-Portsmouth road. It comprised two circular houses, one seven metres in diameter, the other, which contained a hearth, only four metres in diameter. Associated with the houses were three small pits. Unfortunately there was only time for a rescue excavation of this site, but the results are of considerable importance. The settlement site on Little Butser, on the other hand, is the subject of a long-term research excavation.

On all the slopes of Butser Hill are to be found large numbers of trackways, the earliest of which certainly predates the Iron-Age crossdykes and may even be neolithic in origin. A more definite date cannot be given to these trackways, but it is evident that many of them were used intensively for long periods of time. The most deeply hollowed track on the hill is the one which winds its way down across Little Butser into the valley below. Even this track, which clearly was once a main north–south route, is predated by a large number of earlier tracks which can be seen on the scarp slope.

The archaeology of the Little Butser spur has proved to be very complex and, in terms of the discovery of other settlements, disturbing. The distribution of pottery sherds not associated with the field monuments described below suggests quite intensive occupation, but clear surface indications are lacking despite a soil cover of only ten centimetres above the natural chalk rock. Should this pattern be normal, then a vast number of settlement sites may have totally escaped recognition. Apart from the trackways already mentioned, there are several field monuments to be seen on the site. A shallow ditch approximately fifty-nine metres long was dug on the eastern side of the knoll of the spur in the Iron Age. The ditch appears to have been unfinished. In association with the ditch is a dished platform, which excavation indicates was the foundation of a house cut into the side of the hill. A small pillow mound, an artificial rabbit warren, was built on the western side of the spur in the sixteenth or seventeenth century. To the north, also in association with a track, are further earthworks, incidentally in a slope of approximately 30°, of unknown purpose and date.

The main area of the spur has been grazed consistently for many years, perhaps for centuries. Certainly there is little evidence from the excavations carried out to date for a wooded cover. The slopes, on the other hand, have been covered with trees for hundreds of years. The earliest estate maps show their presence and the continuing growth of dogs mercury (*Mercurialis perennis*), blue bells (*Endymion non scriptus*) and wild garlic (*Allium ursinum*) is botanical evidence of ancient woodland. The trees are typical of the chalk lands, being largely ash, yew, oak, hazel and thorn. The hazel was carefully coppiced until twenty years ago to provide material for the hurdle makers of the district.

For the purpose of the project, to build and operate a farm dating to approximately 300 BC, this land area is ideal. Not only does the site have considerable natural resources, but also the added advantage of actually possessing a settlement of about that date. This factor alone lends great authenticity to the whole undertaking, since it is probable that the occupants of that settlement themselves farmed both the spur and the adjacent hill slopes and valley land.

Nonetheless, the challenge of building such a farm is considerable. Not least of the difficulties is the precipitous approach to the site. For six months of every year it is quite impossible to get a vehicle, even a four-wheel-drive Land-Rover, on to the site. This means that a great deal of equipment has to be carried down by hand, or rather, on the back. It is only when faced with such a prospect that one really begins to appreciate weather patterns and their impact upon the human environment.

The development scheme of the project has been carefully designed to have a pilot period of construction and establishment, followed by a very long-term operational period. The need for such a long-term period of at least twenty years lies in the very nature of the research programme. To achieve valid results from an agricultural experiment of any kind, an extended period is required to encompass all the natural variables of weather and land use. The similarity of today's weather to that experienced in the latter part of the Iron Age is well attested by physical evidence discussed later in this book, but more dramatically by the Roman historian Tacitus, who described it as quite foul.

Briefly, the objective was to construct three or four round-houses with barns, byres etc., as the nucleus of the farmstead. A ditch and bank with a palisade fence was to be built around these buildings, and radiating from the farmstead would be a

Courses in kiln manufacture and pottery making are held at the Ancient Farm; here a student is making simple thumb pots from local clay.

number of fields and paddocks with associated tracks and fences. Crops, the prehistoric varieties or the nearest equivalents, were to be grown in the fields, and the appropriate livestock would be brought in to complete the range of activities. Everything had to be accomplished within the strictest scientific limits possible and correlated directly to archaeological evidence. All the round-houses, for example, had to be constructed according to specific excavated house plans. In fact, all buildings of whatever kind which are constructed at the Ancient Farm are based directly upon specific archaeological evidence. This allows a clear focus upon the excavated detail and reminds us that excavation is not simply the collection of artefacts for museums and art historians, but an attempt to understand how people of the past lived and worked.

Once the farmstead, the fields and the livestock have been completed, the purpose is to operate the farm as a working unit and to observe closely the functioning and interaction of the individual elements. The value of the project, both in its intention and the excavation so far accomplished, can be seen at many distinct levels. Perhaps the highest level is the creation of a huge open-air scientific research laboratory, where detailed and precise field experiments are being conducted into prehistoric agriculture, industry and buildings. In addition, research programmes are in operation to devise improved systems of archaeological data retrieval and recording. The results of these experiments will be fundamental in a reappraisal of the Iron Age in southern England. Further, because it is a laboratory, there is facility for other researchers to carry out allied studies in a protected land area. For example, within living memory and therefore for all time, no artificial pesticides or herbicides or even fertilisers have been used on the site. After the beginning of the project in 1972 even the possibility of drift spray has been eliminated, as local farmers have agreed not to spray their land if the wind is blowing towards Little Butser. Indeed, the project site is an ideal area for exploitation for a number of different disciplines, ranging from pollen analysis to earth movement studies.

Clearly the project has a great contribution to make in the field of archaeological interpretation. The research programmes are designed to assess probabilities. By observation of the various processes and structures it has already been proved possible not only to isolate previously unrecognised significant features, but also to reverse generally accepted but unproven theories. Inevitably, the results from the project will serve to make excavation much more cost-effective. Indeed, the total expenditure incurred by the project throughout its six-year life has been less than the cost of a small six-week excavation.

Educationally, the benefits of the project are enormous. For the general public and for schoolchildren it not only explains the work of the archaeologist in the field, but also presents a real working interpretation of the past. Because it sets out to

General view of the research site on Little Butser, Hampshire. In the foreground are the many sheep paddocks and the nucleus of the farmstead. Beyond this is the field system where the prehistoric cereals are grown and studied. Excavation has revealed evidence of occupation of this site in the Iron-Age period to the right of the fields.

explain by experiment, it is better able to underline the difficulties of explanation and increase awareness of the achievements of prehistory. It also provides a way of maintaining skills and knowledge of farming practice which changed little for nearly two thousand years. There is a far greater gap between the agriculture of today and thirty years ago than thirty years ago and 300 BC. The modern generation, for example, has never seen a cereal crop grown without the aid of herbicides and pesticides. Indeed, because of these very aids to modern farming, many common plants of thirty years ago, especially arable weeds, are now either extinct or extremely rare.

The project began in August 1972 with a staff of two: myself and a secretary. Now the staff also includes a farm manager and an interpreter for the newly constructed demonstration area. The initial prospect, to set up a farm with livestock and crops, homes and buildings, was to say the least somewhat daunting. The end result appears to be fairly simple and straightforward. The process, however, has hardly been so. It was like having a huge three-dimensional jig-saw puzzle, some pieces clearly seen, others not yet imagined or even suspected. Which pieces should one create first? What scale of priorities to adopt? Perhaps the most unappreciated aspect of the jig-saw, although quite obvious with the knowledge of hindsight, was that of maintenance and the demands of the farming cycle.

In effect, it is quite simple, if extremely arduous, to construct a field. Once that field has been planted with a crop, a process has been started. Unfortunately, on a field which is not treated with the modern pesticides and herbicides it is not just the planted crop which grows. A profusion of weeds and grasses suddenly appear, and if allowed to flourish unchecked will severely restrict if not completely destroy the planted crop. As recently as the 1930s charlock (*Sinapis arvensis*), a rampant weed of arable fields, was often responsible for the total failure of a crop. Inevitably, therefore, weeding either by hoe or hand becomes necessary. The time spent in maintaining a crop becomes an important factor in the general farm management. Reaping the harvest and its subsequent analysis also take their appropriate portion of time and at the end, after many long hours of effort, all that is left is a field. The three-dimensional jig-saw puzzle inevitably involves the fourth dimension of time.

The first phase of the project, the excavation of the farmstead area, was perhaps the easiest of all. Before any kind of experimental reconstruction work takes place it is vital to

Soay ewe with a lamb less than an hour old.

excavate since the results of this work are themselves significant archaeologically and distortion of results either way is to be avoided at all costs. This excavation was accomplished in the September of 1972 with surprising results. In an area in the saddle of the spur, devoid of any surface indications of occupation, a neolithic scraper and waste flakes (pottery sherds of general Iron-Age type), and a quern were all found in the root-bonded top soil.

In addition, because the excavation was carried out entirely by hand, ephemeral features both geological and archaeological were isolated. This particular excavation, which yielded so much unexpected material, motivated a new research programme devoted to improved techniques for data recovery, a programme that was further stimulated by the standard of the general data available for the Iron-Age period.

The following chapters relate in detail the various elements of the farm which have been collected and created over the past six years. The nucleus of a farm has, in fact, been achieved, and a number of long-term research programmes have been established and are operational. One of these programmes – the experiments devoted to the underground pits, so typical of Iron-Age settlements in southern England and elsewhere – has already produced results which demand a reappraisal of present accepted theories.

So far two round-houses have been built and both, incidentally, have survived the impact of hurricane force winds and torrential rain. A total of five fields has been dug and a major programme of crop yield experiments involving the prehistoric cereals under differing treatments is in process. The livestock holding includes a flock of some twenty Soay sheep maintained in a paddock system and a small herd of long-legged Dexter cattle. Two of these have been trained as a

working pair and form the traction unit of the farm. The Indian Red Jungle Fowl and Old English Game Fowl are kept as domestic fowl. Finally, there is an Exmoor pony and a goat to complete the animal complement.

One of the greatest benefits to emerge from the project so far has been the experience of controlling, training and maintaining the livestock and managing the crop programme. It is by the study of the interaction of all these different elements that a major advance is being made towards understanding the Iron Age – an understanding one could not achieve in any other way. The requirements of the management programme, the provision of winter feed for example, force a reconsideration of the raw archaeological data.

It is by putting together a farm that one learns to ask a completely new range of directly relevant questions. This process alone not only refocusses attention onto the excavation of settlements and pits, but also argues strongly for the future excavation of fields and field boundaries. One major hazard experienced through the life of the project has been that of stock control. There is little evidence of fences in the archaeological record and yet they are of paramount importance. By isolating such areas of enquiry, a carefully constructed programme of research excavation can be mounted to search for specific answers. This aspect alone, the isolation of areas of enquiry, is one of the major contributions made by the Ancient Farm Research Project.

The four-dimensional jig-saw puzzle is far from complete. There are many more pieces still to fit into place. Perhaps because of the very nature of the evidence it will never be finished. However, the present stage of achievement goes some way towards demonstrating the potential of this unique concept and approach.

3 The Houses

Today, whenever experimental archaeology is mentioned, most people immediately think of reconstructed houses. This is quite understandable, especially with prehistoric houses, since they have a tremendous visual impact and are more likely to remain in the memory than an abstruse series of equations or a set of yield figures per hectare. People can identify with a house and enjoy imagining what the domestic arrangements may have been within it. They also enjoy quarrelling with the method of reconstruction adopted and offering alternative views. Every man, it seems, is a thwarted builder. This chapter, therefore, is devoted to the reconstructed houses so far built at the Ancient Farm, and the following chapters will put the house reconstructions into their proper perspective.

At the outset it is vital to stress that the houses and structures built are not necessarily at all like the buildings of the Iron Age. They are simply reconstructions based upon excavated evidence. Each reconstruction is but a physical realisation of one possible interpretation, and for each set of

Maiden Castle house: daub is a mixture of clay, earth, animal hair, grass, hay or any other available binding material. The mixture is puddled with water and plastered onto the basket-work walls. As it dries it cracks. However, once these cracks are filled the wall stays hard. This wall has survived with virtually no attention for more than six years.

archaeological data there are many possible interpretations. The only claim that can reasonably be made is for the validity, not the historical accuracy, of the structure if it stands up and withstands the natural elements for any length of time. The magnificent and elaborately ornate Norwegian wooden houses are a warning to us. They sit upon four or more staddle stones; at best archaeologists may recover only the stones and at worst may miss even the depressions left by them. No reconstructor would imagine the presence of these buildings from such ephemeral evidence.

So far three houses have been built on the Ancient Farm site. Each house is a total experiment in itself but two also play a part in the operation of the farm. Every effort is made to maintain a standard consistency of approach. If, for example, the evidence suggests daubed walls, then all the walls of that house are daubed with the same mixture in the same way. No attempt has been made to insert panels of different wall covering for comparison exercises. The reason for this is straightforward; the houses are round and the weathering pattern will, therefore, differ proportionally, and it is only acceptable to compare like substance with like substance. On rectangular houses, on the other hand, it would be possible and desirable to build any side in two or more walling materials for comparative studies. To pursue this idea still further, if one of the questions asked of a reconstruction is the comparative weathering qualities of different wall materials, the ideal form of structure is an octagon. Each wall of the octagon would have to be set at right-angles to a major point of the compass. The same argument is also true for any future experimental earthwork designed to assess erosion rates and patterns. Consistency of building style is therefore insisted upon.

Surprisingly it is difficult to find good plans of Iron-Age round-houses from the chalk lands of southern Britain. The first reconstruction is based upon a house plan recovered during excavations directed by Sir Mortimer Wheeler on Maiden Castle in Dorset. The evidence consists of a number of post-holes averaging some 30 cm deep surrounding an area of crushed chalk approximately 6 m in diameter, in the centre of which was a further post-hole. Scattered over the general area were fragments of daub – a mixture of clay, soil, straw, animal hair and chalk. To add to this very basic evidence, there is the classical reference (Pytheas) which describes Celtic houses as round with thatched roofs. A further comment, this time by Tacitus, indicates that the normal

Maiden Castle house: the central forked post supports the four major rafters of the roof. The basketwork walls are immensely strong and will sustain considerable pressure.

practice was to use wood in its natural form. This must be in comparison to the Roman practice of squaring-off building timbers.

The Maiden Castle house (each house is named after the site which provided the plan) was built according to this data. The close proximity of the post-holes one to another argued an interwoven or basketwork wall upon which the daub could be plastered. Throughout the reconstruction ash was used for the main timbers and rafters, and hazel was used for the interweaving. The principles of round-house construction are relatively simple to understand. The major purpose throughout is to transfer the lateral thrust exerted by the weight of the

Maiden Castle house: the completed timberwork. The principle of interweaving hazel rods is maintained for the roof itself. Thus a support for the straw thatch is provided. The doorway, as is typical of Iron-Age homes, faces the south-east.

31

roof into circular form around the perimeter of the wall. Consequently it is necessary to complete the circle in its entirety. Inevitably there is great difficulty in achieving this at the doorway. It is one thing to draw an elegant elevation on paper, quite another to achieve it in the solid state. Many penned reconstructions would hardly stand up under their own weight, let alone withstand a stiff wind. Basketwork or interwoven walls are extremely strong. A domestic experiment well worth trying is to stand on the edges of a wicker basket.

The ground plan was carefully repeated with upright poles set in place no more than 30 cm deep into the rock chalk. The ring of poles provided the basis for an interwoven wall 1.50 m high. Incidentally, each post-hole was carefully photographed in colour before the post was placed within it. Thus we have a recorded starting-point for the life of each one, and ultimately will be able to compare the final state with the original and obtain a fully documented life span for the structure as a whole. Thereafter, a comparative record for reference will be available. There was little indication of a doorway in the archaeological data, so the doorway was set to the south-east because a general analysis of doorway orientations of the period suggests that the majority lie in the general quadrant east through south. Hazel rods were interwoven in between the uprights to a height of 1.50 m. At this height a triple hazel-rod wall-plate was tied around the whole circumference of the

Maiden Castle house: the simplest method of thatching was used. Bundles of straw were tied in place in concentric rings around the roof, each succeeding layer overlapping the one before. Over a tonne of straw was required to thatch the roof.

structure and attached to both the inside and outside of the posts. The wall plate was made by tying together three rows of hazel rods in such a way that no two joins were contiguous. Despite this wall-plate, the pressure of the basketwork was sufficient to spring the doorposts slightly outwards at the top.

Wall height and roof pitch represented the first two real problems in the reconstruction process. The evidence so far had been followed exactly, and one could be confident of approaching the original wall type. Unfortunately, we had little or no indication of wall height beyond the occasional door-post or doorway from stone structures of that time. The small Celtic stone houses of the Portuguese and Spanish coastlands and the brochs of Scotland suggest a doorway height of 1.50 m. In fact, it is a comfortable height to adopt, allowing headroom for a modern man of average height, 1.80 m, just inside the house. As yet we have insufficient evidence to postulate an average height for Iron-Age man, though his diet was at least as nutritious as our own. For the roof pitch our problems were even greater. For a thatched roof the minimum functional pitch is 45°. Thatched cottages traditionally have a roof pitch of between 45° and 55°. For a cone-shaped roof a pitch of 45° is mathematically most attractive. At this angle there is less lateral thrust on a point of moment, major thrust being exerted at 22.5° and 67.5°. Also, since the roof is to be thatched and a minimum of 45° is required, this also represents the minimum roof area to be thatched. By increasing the angle, we increase the area.

For this reconstruction the post-hole found at the centre of the house plan was taken to be the proof for a central support to the roof. A forked pole measuring 4.50 m to the notch of the fork was selected and set in place. Thereafter four main rafters 5.50 m long were laid into the notch. The distance from the notch to the wall is only 4.25 m but an overlap is necessary at the roof apex. An eave of just under a metre was allowed. The method adopted for fixing the rafters to the wall posts, which protruded some 20 cm above the wall plate, was a simple friction plate joint. In order to join two round timbers together it is necessary to cut two flat faces at the point of contact. Two cuts with an axe were sufficient. The joint was then lashed together with rawhide. The basic advantage of using rawhide over twine or other natural fibres like Old Man's Beard (*Clematis vitalba*) is that as it dries out it shrinks slightly drawing the timbers even more tightly together.

The second major difficulty encountered in building cone-shaped roofs is at the apex. Very quickly the timbers choke this area completely, and unless one is prepared to distort the building line of the roof, a dangerous principle with thatch, it is necessary to provide a subsidiary support for the majority of the rafters. This is done by attaching a ring beam of horizontal timbers to the outside of the four principal rafters approximately 1.50 m from the apex. For the Maiden Castle house four timbers were used making a rectilinear ring beam. All the remaining rafters were lashed to this ring beam and to the wall uprights. Initially, the roof structure with only four major rafters in position is quite weak, but as each succeeding rafter is lashed into place the roof steadily gains in strength. In effect, the increasing number of timbers reduces the breaking distance of the supporting ring. For example it is comparatively easy to break a timber over 2 m long and some 8 cm in diameter. It is another matter to break that timber when it is only 30 cm long.

The final stage of the timberwork was to interlace between the rafters further hazel rods, again adding significantly to the strength of the structure. The building throughout is constructed under tension. Once it is completed, the wood sets in place and dries. A test I apply to all reconstruction for which I am responsible is to walk up one side of the roof and down the other. This exerts over a tonne per square metre, a pressure the structure will never have to withstand from the natural elements.

The ultimate processes are the thatching, followed by the daubing. The former was carried out using wheat straw tied into bundles, traditionally called yealms, and then tied to the roof working upwards from the eaves in concentric circles. Just over one tonne of straw was used to thatch this house.

The daub on the other hand was much more straightforward. The recipe used for this house was as follows: 3.5 tonnes of clay, 3.5 tonnes of earth, 40 bales of straw, the hair from 40 pigs, sundry brambles, grass, hay, roots and other vegetable matter. It was mixed with water to a plastic consistency, and then applied liberally by hand to the basketwork walls both inside and out, making sure that the daub was well keyed in place. In fact, it took quite some time to prepare and apply the daub with a work force of only two or three people. Subsequent reconstructions of greater proportions have been successfully daubed in a day by twenty or more workers. However, the first application is not the final one. The daub dries out and cracks, and it is necessary to fill these cracks carefully with a similar mixture. Once the wall has been completely plastered and filled it requires little attention for

some years. In fact, this house, which was completed in 1973, has required less maintenance per annum than the average time of two weekends spent by D.I.Y. house owners.

There are a number of different kinds of daub and similar walling material, like cob and clunch. Some have admixtures of cow dung, others have varying quantities of clay, earth and chalk, but in reality they are all fairly similar. One variety, a mixture of cow dung and chalk or earth, is extremely interesting. It was a common walling material in Dorset and Wiltshire in past centuries and, provided the top of the wall is protected and the sides washed with lime, such walls will last a considerable time. It may well be that many prehistoric houses were plastered with such a mixture, since in a vast majority of cases there is no evidence whatsoever of clay deposits which would be expected from daubed walls.

The completed Maiden Castle house is but one interpretation of a set of archaeological data. Even immediately after its completion, it was possible to prove that the central post-hole was unlikely to have been used by a central roof support. A house of this size simply does not require such a support. Alternative interpretations for a post in this position are not hard to suggest. For example, it could have been a potstand, that is a post with a number of pegs set into it at an upward angle upon which inverted pots could be stored; or it could have supported a mezzanine floor in the roof area for storage purposes; or it could have supported a cauldron over a hearth;

Maiden Castle house: the completed structure. Set on the exposed spur of Little Butser this house has withstood hurricane force winds with impunity. Aerodynamically its shape is ideal. At no time is a flat surface presented against the elements.

35

or it could have been a pivot for room dividers. What is lacking is more precise archaeological data from the floor area of the house.

Naturally, the life cycle of the house is being carefully monitored, and it is worth reporting that already it has successfully withstood several hurricane force winds and a winter when over 1.20 m of rain fell within six months without damage or leaks. This is more than can be said for some modern structures! One particularly interesting change has already taken place. During the winter months the house is often used for storing grain and hay. Inevitably this attracts the attention of rats, which have tunnelled beneath the walls. Around parts of the circumference of the house the rats, by their activities, have palpably altered the 'archaeological evidence' and instead of post-holes we now have 'gulleys'. It is relevant to note that a number of Iron-Age houses are indicated by gulleys rather than post-holes. A further observation has been the absence to date of any drip trench forming under the eaves. In fact the reverse has happened, with a luxuriant growth of grass. By contrast, the doorway area is now marked by a shallow depression caused by walking in and out of the house in wet weather and splashing away material. This particular observation aided the identification of threshold areas at a recent excavation where there was no other clear indication.

The Balksbury house, based upon evidence from recent excavation at Balksbury near Andover in Hampshire, is quite different in concept and execution. The evidence consists simply of a circle of post-holes exactly 9.10 m in diameter, the post-holes being an average 1.92 m apart. On the eastern side there was a further set of four post-holes, rectangular in plan, suggesting an annexe or porch to the structure. Since the area of the excavation was scraped by a machine, there was no further evidence beyond the post-hole pattern. The average depth of the post-holes was 24 cm and the probable diameter of the posts was 15 cm. It must be emphasised that this post-hole pattern does not necessarily belong to a house. Such a pattern could represent a number of other perfectly good alternatives. Indeed, an alternative version has been built at the Ancient Farm and is described later in this chapter.

Following the hypothesis that the pattern represents a house, another reconstruction was built in 1974 and 1975. Because the posts are set so far apart, it was impossible to consider any kind of basketwork or interwoven wall, and one was forced into the realms of timber frame construction. The

Maiden Castle house was deliberately made in the simplest way possible, despite our knowledge of the consummate carpentry skills of the Iron Age. For the Balksbury house more sophisticated joinery was necessary. As for the Maiden Castle house, posts were set into previously photographed post-holes and packed into place. Thereafter, tenons were cut onto the top of each post and a wall plate of curved timbers was morticed piecemeal into place. Each element of the wall-plate was carefully selected for its curve and was jointed to the next element with a pegged scarf-joint. An error, recognised inevitably with hindsight, was made by including the porch as integral to the structure and thus breaking the basic ring construction of the wall plate.

Since there was no evidence for any central support for the roof apex, a free span of over 9 m had to be constructed. The same angle of 45° was chosen for the roof pitch, and rafters of ash were gathered accordingly. Mathematically, the roof needed to be braced at a point one third of the way down the rafters from the apex. This suggested a pentagonal ring beam, one element of which had to be at right angles to the porch area. To construct the roof, three rafters were notched and drilled at the point where they were to sit on the wall-plate and then tied loosely together at the apex. All three rafters were then raised together into a vertical position in the centre of the house, and then the foot of each one was slowly walked outwards making a tripod. Finally, each leg of the tripod was raised into position and propped before being finally pegged. The whole operation was carried out by a man and a girl. Thereafter two more rafters were added into the 'cross-trees' provided by the first tree.

The pentagonal ring beam was prefabricated on the ground and hauled into position with a rope. Only at this moment was

The framework of the Balksbury house. Unlike the Maiden Castle house, its strength is drawn from the continuous wall plate attached to the uprights with simple mortice and tenon joints.

The skeleton of the roof comprises five main rafters. The pentagonal ring beam is set one-third down the slant height of the roof.

The wall panels are made of split hazel rods. The thin stakes of each panel are simply wedged in place.

a ladder introduced to secure the ring beam in place. (Ladders were known and used in the Iron Age.)

The successive stages of the reconstruction thereafter were quite logical and straightforward. The remaining rafters were pegged into position and lashed to the ring beam. Finally, split hazel rods were tied in concentric rings about 40 cm apart onto the rafters to form the purlins to support the thatch. The purlins acted as a multiple number of ring beams, adding substantially to the strength of the structure.

The wall frames were filled with split hazel panels and daubed as in the Maiden Castle house. Finally the roof was thatched with approximately three tonnes of reed. For neither reconstruction have I given details of the time spent on building although these data are kept. The purpose is to avoid calculations being made on a false premise. The time record is extremely interesting, but it begs entirely the question of skill. Both houses are experiments, and as such we are seeking ways of interpreting archaeological data. If such reconstructions are accepted as valid structures, we are now in a position to build again, having acquired the basic skill and knowledge, and then

The completed cone: split hazel rods have been interwoven in and out of all the rafters.

A reconstructed Celtic axe and a bundle of hazel rods.

The completed houses:
the porch of the Balksbury
house is at too shallow a
pitch and this major design
fault led to the dismantling
of the structure.

the time taken would be a useful factor. Experiments which
record time spent by unskilled operatives on skilled tasks, and
use such information, are valueless in complex calculations.

All the tools used in the reconstruction of both houses were
available to Iron-Age man, although we used modern versions
of them. A full-scale carpenter's tool-kit existed in the mid-
Bronze Age as far as we can tell at the present. Certainly all the
joinery used in the Balksbury house can be shown from not
just the Iron Age, but also the Neolithic period.

As I mentioned above there is justifiable doubt whether the
ground plan upon which the Balksbury house is based is
necessarily a house at all. Even as a house, there is no real need
to utilise the four post-holes on the eastern side as an integral
porch. These could well be interpreted as a pair of racks, or a

Patterns of post-holes do not always indicate structures. Here two posts support a stack of thatching straw. The horizontal timber holds the straw in place.

small shed, or any number of things. Consequently, it was decided to build another structure, important within the organisation of the farm, based upon this evidence and again including the four-post-holed annexe. It so happens that the average distance between the upright posts correlates to the average length of a sheep hurdle. Furthermore, the annexe makes a splendid double isolation pen in which the sheep could be handled individually. Hence a very sound sheepfold was built on exactly the same data. The reason for double hurdling is because the Soay sheep are quite capable of jumping 1.8 m from virtually a standing start. During the periods when the fold is not in use the hurdles are taken down and stored.

This exercise demonstrates the value of the experimental approach in providing a multiplicity of interpretations. It has been said that experiments can make no positive statement about archaeological data. This may be so, but it can definitely prove negatives and further underline the need for both flexibility of interpretation and validity tests.

This final section on houses is devoted to a purely hypothetical structure. One of the clearly stated aims of the Research Project is its educational capacity. In fulfilling this role courses are regularly held throughout the year for students of all ages. During one such course in the winter of 1972–73 the subject under discussion was devoted to the solitary post-hole and its potential significance in settlement patterns. The theory put forward for empirical testing was that an isolated post-hole could indicate the presence of a house. During the course such a house was constructed, the *caveat* being that the only evidence it could have archaeologically was a single post hole.

The house, some 6 m in diameter, was made with turf walls just under a metre thick and a metre high. A central forked post was set in position and supported the major rafters. A

rectilinear ring-beam, exactly similar to the one in the Maiden Castle house, supported the supplementary rafters. All the rafter ends were simply laid on top of the turf wall. Hazel rods interwoven between the rafters formed the support for the turf roof. The pitch of this roof, because it was made of turf, was low at approximately 30°.

A house based upon a solitary post-hole. The rafters are supported by the central pole at the apex and by the turf wall. The roof necessarily has to be very strong to support the turf cover.

The construction details need not detain us here, other than to explain that a turf house with a turf roof needs a fire permanently burning inside to maintain the roof structure. The turves are put on in two layers – the first grass downwards, and the second, sealing the joints of the first layer, grass uppermost. The object of the fire is to provide sufficient temperature in the roof space to encourage grass growth and therefore rooting of the upper layer. The roots thus hold the roof together. It was impossible to maintain a permanent fire within this house and it was decided to allow it to collapse and to monitor the collapse over a number of years. Within months the roof fell in and the wall began to deteriorate. As present it looks rather like a robbed-out round-barrow.

This was a straightforward experiment but with considerable significance, because it argues for increased care in excavation. Houses made with turf walls and roofs are not unlikely in the prehistoric period, although none has yet been isolated. Nonetheless, there are ethnographic examples of such houses, both round and rectangular. With normal excavation procedure one will locate only the post-holes, and even these are not vital to the construction since the posts

43

could equally well be wedged in position on the ground surface or even placed on stone supports. The secret of the identification of such houses would seem to lie in the discovery of the distribution patterns of occupation debris.

For a turf house such as the one described above one can hypothesize a number of probable distribution patterns – for example, occupation debris spread over a circular area, with or without a central post-hole, bounded by a sterile perimeter band with further debris spread beyond. An alternative would be a circular area as before, but sterile with occupation debris beyond it. Perhaps there may be a shallow depression, a possible threshold, with a particular concentration of occupational material fanning away from it. Further patterns and combinations of them are not difficult to propose. The real point at issue is the great need for more precise excavation and the exact recording of each and every artefact in its find position in case such patterns should emerge. In chapter seven I have outlined an experiment designed to examine sherd movement under present agricultural conditions. As yet the

The completed turf round-house. After destruction and ploughing the only evidence which might survive is a solitary post-hole.

44

argument that plough damage is sufficient excuse to rip apart a site in order to recover the objects as quickly as possible is largely unproven. Many sites are sufficiently deeply buried to be beyond immediate risk. At all events it seems not only desirable but necessary to excavate cubic centimetre by cubic centimetre, and to record just as minutely.

In this connection, while we can recognise the presence of houses we still have no real evidence as to their functions. We do not yet know, for example, whether a round-house is a full-scale domestic unit or merely one element of a unit. Perhaps more careful excavation will lead to clearer identification of function.

Fig. 1 Ground plan of the Balksbury house.

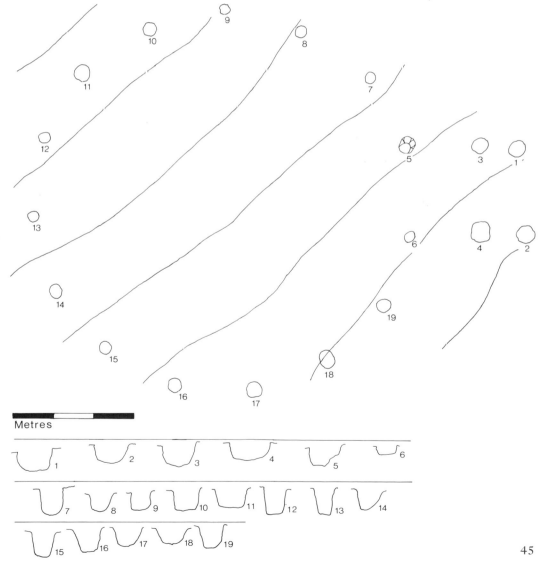

45

Soay ram. These athletic animals are capable of jumping nearly two metres.

4 *The Farm Livestock*

This particular element of the farm is the most difficult of all to reconstruct. Our evidence comes from the two basic sources of excavation and documentation. The former is inevitably non-representative and the latter of doubtful value. Bones are the hardware of interpretation but unfortunately bones have many other uses once the meat has been removed and their survival qualities are not particularly good. A glance at a number of appendices attached to excavation reports is explanation enough. There are numerous dull and surprisingly short lists of bones, many of which are ascribed to a strange sheep/goat species simply because it is extremely difficult to distinguish the individual species. There are notable exceptions to this system of species lists where attempts have been made, most successfully, to consider the skeletal remains in terms of the muscle, meat and skin they originally supported. In this way we have learned considerably more about prehistoric livestock.

It is interesting to reflect on what may have happened to the bone waste from Iron-Age settlements. The majority of bones must have been eaten by dogs and pigs. The well-fed labrador of modern times is quite capable of reducing large long bones to insignificant crumbs, and a similar result would have been achieved, probably even more quickly, by a prehistoric hunting dog. Pigs will utterly destroy all bones, an ability exploited by not a few murderers who have wished to rid themselves of an embarrassing cadaver. Humans destroy bones by boiling them, especially marrow bones, which provide stock for soups and broths. Indeed, it is remarkable that any bones have survived at all from the domestic economy, particularly after two thousand years in acid soils.

Distinct from their nutritional qualities, bones also had great value as the raw material for the manufacture of tools. Perhaps the greatest exploitation of bone for tools belongs to the Stone Age, but nonetheless it was still used on a fairly large scale throughout prehistory, including the Iron Age. Pins, toggles, needles, burins and other small tools are quite common. Occasionally bones used as thatchers' needles, awls, handles, weaving combs and the like have implications beyond the material itself.

Here our basic concern is the animals such bones represent, whether they are domestic or feral and what part they may have played within an agricultural economy. At the Ancient

Farm, of course, identification is only the first step. The next and almost unanswerable question is how they were kept. Perhaps definitive answers will ultimately emerge from the research programmes in the sense that archaeological comparison standards may be provided, but more likely a number of realistic variables will be forthcoming. It is one thing to think that a certain system of husbandry was practised, it is quite another to know such a system is actually practicable. Interpretation of archaeological data is a most difficult exercise and fraught with dangers of oversimplification. Two examples drawn from ethnography may illustrate these difficulties. It is quite common to think of a farm as a compact physical unit where time and effort are correlated economically, but this reasonable supposition is not necessarily true and is a dangerous basis upon which to construct models of landscape utilisation. The important factors ignored are land ownership, tenurial rights and inheritance laws. To this day in parts of Spain peasant farming not dissimilar from the supposed Celtic or Roman systems is still practised, but because of the inheritance laws one farmer may have small parcels of land separated by several kilometres. This is most uneconomic in terms of labour and time, but the resistance to reorganisation of land-holding is considerable. The example makes nonsense of the much-used premise that a man will not walk more than one kilometre to work. It also underlines the

The Dexter cattle, similar in size and power to the extinct Celtic Shorthorn have been trained to the yoke and form the traction unit of the farm.

Furrows made with a simple ard, which stirs up the soil rather than inverts it. In effect only the topsoil is cultivated, which accords exactly with the most modern methods of farming.

flaw in the system of infield (an intensive agricultural area around the farmstead) and outfield (an occasional grazing and catch-cropping area). The practice of farming is the utilisation of the best land for a particular purpose, and the best land for intensive agriculture may well not be adjacent to the farmstead itself.

Again, in interpretation one always seeks to regularise when in reality regularity is not the norm. A very simple example is the way of yoking together cattle to pull ploughs and carts. In brief, there are two basic ways, neck yoking and horn yoking. Good cases can be made in favour of either system. It would be simpler for the archaeologist to have just one system, and it is tempting to think that if there are two systems then they could easily represent regional differences. In fact, in most countries where cattle are still used, both ways exist side by side and are the subject of hot dispute locally from their advocates.

The cattle bones of the Iron Age have been identified as belonging to the extinct shorthorn (*bos longifrons*), a small undeveloped rangy animal. It was the progenitor of the Kerry cattle of Ireland and the Welsh Black cattle. The Highland cattle are clear examples of a similar breed to the extinct shorthorn, being small and rangy, able to do well on mean pasture and withstand the winter on poor food supplies. However, at the Farm it was decided to use Dexter cattle as the principal stock. The Dexter cattle were originally bred from the Kerry cattle in the last century, the intention being to produce a very small 'house cow'. As a breed they have been quite successful especially with small farms and holdings in Ireland and in the border country. They are capable of living off very poor pasture and still thriving, giving an adequate milk yield for a family, and being most amenable creatures. Often a Dexter cow is more of a pet than a farm animal. The breed, however, is a little unstable, and occasionally it reverts back slightly to the Kerry. The animals selected for the farm have, in fact, reverted slightly in that they have longer legs than the standard small Dexter. As such they correlate extremely well with the bone evidence, and the long-legged Dexter is thought to be very representative in shoulder height, body weight and general appearance to the Celtic shorthorn.

Modern cattle, although kept under close control, retain the independent temperament of wild animals. They are intensely curious and will readily approach humans, but that does not mean that they are at all tractable. It requires a long period of careful handling and training before cows or steers can be useful beyond a source of milk and meat. We think that in the Iron Age cattle, specifically cows, were used as the main traction unit in the farming economy. Our intention, there-fore, has been to train a pair of long-legged Dexters to the yoke in order to use them for ploughing and carting purposes on the farm.

The implications even for this simple intention are far-reaching. If they were used for traction (and there is no reason to assume otherwise), how were they kept? Clearly they were special animals, and it is most unlikely that they were kept in a similar way to modern practice. Ethnography here is most helpful. In many countries throughout the world we find cattle are used for farmwork. The cow is preferred to the steer simply because one can also get a milk yield. In nearly every case the cattle receive special treatment. They either live in the same building as the humans or else in special byres. Feeding, too, is specialised. The animals can be tethered out for certain periods each day, or else food is brought to them, a system called zero grazing. This latter system, not a modern concept at all, has the advantage that the quantity and quality of feed can be carefully monitored. What happened in the Iron Age in Britain? As yet we have no evidence from the houses that cattle shared human habitation. This is in direct contrast to the Continental long-home evidence, where stalls for cattle have been clearly identified. Perhaps they were kept in byres, the evidence being the four- and five-post-hole structures.

Perhaps they did share the accommodation inside round-houses. More careful excavation and chemical analyses of floor areas may yet provide the answer.

One major implication of which we can be sure is that the maintenance of cattle inevitably meant the making and storing of hay and possibly silage as well. In terms of farm organisation, this is a most important element, since it implies the provision of a hay crop and the necessary land allocation for it.

Few yokes have survived, but those that have, both neck and horn types, are most interesting. The distance between the tie positions where the yoke is attached to the animal is often a metre. This argues, from practical experience, that the animals had quite large spread horns and the yokes were designed to keep the heads apart.

Evidence for Iron-Age ploughs in this country is extremely limited, and we have to look to the finds of wooden ploughs in the Danish peat bogs. In reality they are properly ards rather than ploughs in that they are not fitted with a mould board, which inverts the soil. The ard is technically a spike which scores a furrow in the ground and only stirs the soil. Nonetheless, the ard is a complex and efficient tool, the direct modern parallel being the chisel plough. In this country many metal tips or socks have been found which are thought to have been fitted over the end of the wooden spike.

Our evidence for the use of ards in Britain largely consists of score marks. These scores, called ard marks, are found as early as the beginning of the Bronze Age. Some experiments have already been carried out with reconstructed ploughs in order to discover more about the nature of these ard marks and also to test the efficiency and the effect of the ard. Preliminary results from experiments carried out by the author some years ago suggest that, contrary to accepted opinion, the simple wooden ard is capable of dealing with not only the light soils of the chalk and limestone uplands, but also the heavy clays and loams of the valleys, a finding recently supported when ard marks were identified on heavy clay in the south-west. The need for metal socks to protect the wooden spike of the ard was also underlined, since the ploughing of just half a hectare was sufficient to wear away 2.5 cm of solid, seasoned, oak spike.

There is need for much more research into soil flow, creation of ard marks, minimal cultivation, comparative effect on earthworm populations and resultant arable yield figures before we will be able to understand this aspect of prehistoric farming thoroughly.

The basic requirement before any of the above can be

achieved is a pair of trained cattle of the right size and power ratio. The Dexter cattle at the Ancient Farm will fulfil this basic requirement and in addition, by being part of the organisation of the Farm, will aid further insight into the problems of husbandry.

Finally, an inference made from the study of the Celtic field systems still available as field monuments is that such fields, averaging approximately 0.13 hectares, represent areas capable of being dealt with within a day. This, too, will be subject to careful testing as will the production of lynchets or low banks which occur on the lower edges of such fields on sloping ground.

The existence of another kind of archaeological field monument, the so-called 'ranch-boundaries' which often contain large tracts of land, suggests the maintenance of cattle herds. This interpretation is possibly supported by the classical reference concerning the export of leather from this country in the immediate pre-Roman period. It is an attractive proposition and in no way detracts from the above discussion. It is quite possible that in the Iron Age there were different types of farming as there are today, and ranching is a likely alternative. There is another interpretation that could be offered for these ranch boundaries. Excavations of settlement sites regularly recover large quantities of red and roe deer bones, proportionally many more than cattle bones. Perhaps the ranch boundaries represent part of a system of deer farming, a type of farming which is being reintroduced today. The principle is one of containment with annual round-ups and culling. For this the ranch boundary of linear ditch and bank with presumed fence is not dissimilar from the nineteenth-century method of deer-park boundaries.

Evidence suggests that pigs were kept domestically as well as hunted. The European wild boar (*Sus scrofa*) still exists today and is also a modern quarry of the hunt. However, the domestic pigs of prehistory are extinct, and an interesting breeding experiment was carried out under the aegis of the Ancient Farm. In order to back-breed to the original pigs the ideal pairing is the European wild boar and the Tamworth pig. The latter is the oldest extant variety of pig which has no Asiatic influence in its genetic structure. Such a pairing was arranged and resulted in a litter of stripey piglets. This exercise was in no way a serious breeding experiment, since for such a project a minimum number of a hundred breeding pairs are required. Rather, it was an exploratory test. The progeny were fairly small and rangy and almost impossible to contain;

extremely fleet of foot, they could easily outrun a dog and on occasions did so. The interest in pigs at the Farm is largely concerned with pig pannage and the possibility of locating such pannage archaeologically. Unfortunately, financial restrictions and the cost of foodstuff has meant the postponement of the pig-pannage experiments until a later date. Also, the intention is to study the pig as a potential plough. It is possible, for example, to use a herd of pigs in such a way as to prepare and manure a seed bed, clean up after harvest, and never actually employ a plough at all. The only human input is concerned with planting, hoeing and reaping.

It must be made clear at this juncture that the business of the Ancient Farm is not involved with back-breeding experiments at all. It is too complex a process and of questionable value. Unless the animals are actually available, then the nearest equivalent is employed as in the case of the Dexter cattle.

For sheep, on the other hand, we are much more fortunate in that for the past two millennia the Soay breed has survived virtually unaltered on the St Kilda Islands off the north-west coast of Scotland. Their skeletal structure is extremely similar to excavated sheep bones, and it is not unreasonable to think of them as the sheep of prehistory in this country. They look remarkably like goats, leading of course to the confusion in the skeletal evidence; they run like deer and will jump over 1.8 metres; they are impervious to dog control, a factor possibly brought about by their survival in the wild state, but which may be a natural characteristic. To my knowledge, no modern Soay flock has been successfully controlled with dogs. The wool is plucked and not sheared, with an annual yield of

In winter the Soays need to be fed. This flock has been carefully bred from wild stock brought from the Island of Hirta, one of the St Kildan Islands off the north-west coast of Scotland.

53

approximately one kilo per animal per year. Scottish folklore suggests that a flock of twenty such sheep is needed to provide a family of five with adequate clothing. Lambing usually takes place late in April and May. The Soay sheep deliver the largest lamb in proportion to body size of any sheep. The average ewe weighs only 20–25 kilograms and so they were probably kept more for their wool than for their meat.

The problems of sheep husbandry at the Farm have to be viewed in terms of the natural characteristics of the Soay. They have been kept in paddocks commensurate in size to the normal Celtic fields and rotated on a weekly basis. During the winter they are more tractable as long as supplementary feeding is carried out, but in summer they revert quickly to self-sustainment. Adequate fencing is extremely difficult to arrange. They have a much greater territorial consciousness than modern sheep and will range quite readily over forty square kilometres. If one can read back these characteristics into the Iron Age the vision of shepherds wandering about the high downs with their flocks (the favourite principle of transhumance) perhaps requires a little revision. It seems more likely that the shepherd followed if not pursued his flock, and the danger to the cereal crops from the wide-ranging Soays may have prohibited widespread grazing.

Goats, too, were kept in the farms of the Iron Age and were similar in appearance to the sheep. In contrast to the latter, the goat is a good milk provider and easier to feed and domesticate. Indeed, because it is a browsing rather than a grazing animal, it can fulfil many useful functions. The practice is known, for example, of turning goats out onto an area destined for a hay crop, so that they will browse out all the unwanted weeds like thistles and yet do little or no damage to the hay crop. They can be used for secondary clearance of land in the same way. Unfortunately, the Old English goat, which by description fits the evidence fairly closely, is extremely rare if not already extinct. The parable of separating the sheep from the goats has considerably more impact once one has seen the close resemblance between Soay sheep and old fashioned goats.

Bones of horses are regularly found, especially the skulls. From the nature of the places where they have been found, the frequency of decorated bits and harness attachments and the classical references, especially the passages in Caesar's War Commentaries, it would seem that the horse was a status symbol of some importance in the Iron Age. It is almost impossible to identify the direct descendant of the Celtic horse, which was small, very tough and swift, but the Exmoor pony seems to fulfil many of the requirements. Consequently, a pony of this breed is kept at the Ancient Farm in order to observe the interaction of maintenance problems in association with the other livestock.

The evidence of domestic fowl is at present fairly slight, possibly because bird bones survive least well of all. Some have been found and indicate that the most likely bird is the Indian Red Jungle Fowl, which is considered to be the predecessor of all domestic fowl. It has its origins in India and the Far East and could well have been present in this country in the early Iron Age. Alternatively, the Old English Game Fowl, a further link in the evolutionary chain, which culminates with the modern chicken, may have been used at this time. Both species are kept at the Farm.

Actual identification of species and the postulation that they were domesticated is one thing; their maintenance, on the other hand, focuses attention on the realities of farm organisation and asks specific questions of the archaeological record. What kind of chicken houses were constructed, if any? Are some of the four-post structures to be considered as chicken houses, since protection of some kind is vital against the natural predators like the stoat and fox? Ethnography certainly supplies a number of such parallels. It is also worth considering one further implication of keeping chickens, in relation to post-hole evidence. Chickens cheerfully scratch about and often will concentrate their activities around a specific post. In the course of time they can enlarge a perfectly respectable tailored post-hole into a large post-pit. This simple activity alone distorts the evidence to such an extent that any arrangement of post-holes on the basis of similarity of type is suspect.

Geese and ducks, too, may have been kept within the farmstead. Of the possible species the grey lag goose and the mallard duck are the most likely. Bones of both types of bird have been found which are slightly larger than those of the normal wild birds. This factor, it must be emphasised, is certainly not conclusive.

In this section, I have outlined some of the animals which are maintained at the Ancient Farm and the implications of their management, as well as referring to other potential domesticates which need to be considered in the future. The purpose throughout is twofold, to consider the individual animal, its needs and management problems and to view the interaction of such management within the complex of the Farm as a whole.

Emmer wheat.

5 The Crops

Ear of Emmer wheat, the symbol of the Farm, from a gold stater of Cunobelin, struck at Camulodunum (Colchester). $2\frac{1}{2} \times$ *actual size*.

Crop husbandry is one of the major activities of the research project and it is in this area, perhaps, that the greatest contribution can be made to our better understanding of the prehistoric period. Our knowledge of prehistoric plants comes principally from careful study and identification of carbonised organic material recovered by excavation. Major advances in this subject, known as paleobotany, have been made in the last thirty years, due mainly to the work of F. Haelbeck.

Essentially the process is the identification of seeds and parts of plants that have been turned into charcoal, thus preserving both shape and form. Occasionally extravagant claims have been based upon such evidence, suggesting that the analysis of percentages could establish preferred crops and sometimes even the rotation of crops. It is worth remembering that at present the greatest single quantity of carbonised cereal remains does not exceed 50 kilograms, and the majority of finds can be numbered in tens rather than thousands of seeds.

For carbonisation to take place at all, it is necessary that reducing conditions exist within a fire, that is, at least part of the fire must burn without oxygen. Such conditions exist occasionally in the heart of a bonfire provided it is left alone, sometimes inside a pit or hole and perhaps inside an oven as the result of over-roasting. Carbonisation regularly takes place when a building is burned down once the roof falls in and oxygen is excluded from the fire. It will inevitably take place inside a charcoal burner's clamp or a potter's pit clamp. The possible sources of carbonised seed, therefore, are relatively few and only one, roasting, can be argued to be deliberate. The location of the above sources, which are not exclusive, are all regularly to be found within the farmyard or homestead. Indeed, virtually all discoveries of carbonised cereals come from settlement or occupation sites and not the surrounding fields.

A further factor which we must take into consideration, therefore, is the nature of the farm or settlement site. We can reasonably accept that prehistoric economy was basically agricultural in nature, since from analysis of the carbonised seeds we know that a variety of crops were cultivated, some of which are grown to this day, and some of which have been superseded by more efficient plants. However, the carbonised

Fire may have been used to purify a pit. After firing the majority of the waste grain is totally burned but some is carbonised.

57

seeds have invariably been found within the settlement, to which all the harvest was brought and where seeds could easily be mixed up during threshing and storage. Let us imagine a potential process leading to the discovery of carbonised cereal. Barley, wheat and oats were harvested on a prehistoric farm and threshed on a barn floor. Afterwards the chaff and seeds left behind were gathered into a bonfire and left to burn. The remains of the bonfire, the very heart of it, contained a few thousand carbonised seeds. The chance boot which delivered a dispersing kick, a cartwheel rolling over it, a cow shambling through it, all may have served to spread the remains far and wide. Just a few seeds came to rest beside a post and filtered their way into the post-hole to be discovered two millennia later. By no stretch of the imagination could they be used to indicate all the crops grown at that farm for that one season, let alone the duration of the life of the farm. Nor could they indicate the function of the building to which the post-hole belonged, since they had arrived by accident. They simply indicate the presence of those seeds on that particular site.

It is therefore better by far that at present carbonised seeds are used only as indicators of potential crops. Those seeds which are occasionally discovered inside the ubiquitous pit of the Iron-Age period have perhaps more significance, but only in so far as they may have been deliberately stored. In chapter six a discussion of grain storage in underground silos includes the incidence of such seeds.

The evidence from carbonised seeds allows us to make the assumption that a number of different cereals were grown in the Iron Age in Britain and that of these varieties, two wheats, Emmer (*Triticum dicoccum*) and Spelt (*Triticum spelta*), were quite common. Further evidence for their presence in this period is supplied by classical references and coin inscriptions. Indeed, the emblem of the Farm, a stylised ear of Emmer wheat, is inspired by a late Iron-Age coin.

The first wheat grown in prehistory was Einkorn (*Triticum monococcum*). This has played a major part in man's change from a hunter-gatherer into a settled farmer. The wild variety, *Triticum monococcoides*, as well as the domesticated variety, still grows in Asia Minor to this day. At the Farm we have carried out several trials with Einkorn, all of which have had remarkable and unexpected results.

Initially, the purpose was to increase our holding of seed, in order to be in a position to run extensive comparative yield tests in different situations and soil types. However, the

growing process itself gave valuable insight into the plants'
competitive characteristics. The few seeds we had at the
beginning allowed a small plot of one hundred square metres
to be planted, with just a few seeds left over in case of disaster.

The early days of the Ancient Farm Project were extremely
busy and keeping a rhythm with the seasons of that first year
was most difficult. The spring planting of all the crops was
achieved just in time and all proceeded according to plan
except that the Einkorn was late to show. Indeed the grass
regeneration was such that we were virtually resigned to
failure. However, that other disaster of small-scale farming,
the rabbit, struck in late May. The rabbit, thought to have
been introduced into this country by the Normans is, of
course, not allowed in Iron-Age farming and as far as possible
every effort is made to exclude this unwanted variable from
the research programme. However, Einkorn not only proved
unpalatable to the rabbit, but also began to compete successfully with the surrounding grass. In early June it was possible
to hoe between the rows of Einkorn merely by identifying a
colour difference in the herbage, and thereby its survival
chances improved still further. By harvest time a most
creditable crop had appeared. As with all the cereals grown at
Butser, the harvest was taken in such a way as to allow a
statistical evaluation of the bulk yield. A number of squares,
selected with the use of random number tables, were carefully
harvested and all the ears weighed. The resultant overall
figure of over 1.4 tonnes to the hectare was remarkable. In
successive years, and most notably in 1976 when a period of
sustained drought severely crippled all other cereals, the yield
from the Einkorn experimental crops has never fallen below
this first yield figure.

One implication of the tremendous competitive capacity of
Einkorn, is the possibility that at the very beginning of cereal
farming, it formed a minor part of man's activities. For
example, it is possible to plant Einkorn in a prepared seed bed
in the spring and then leave it until harvest time. In the
interim period the hunting of game and gathering of wild
fruits could have gone on as before, but with the insurance
policy of a winter supply of food. From our experience, it
escapes the attention of birds until it is fully ripe and seems to
be beneath the dignity of deer, who prefer Emmer and Spelt
shoots. A simple fence of brushwood would have been
sufficient to deter any other grazing animals. Clearly, further
research is necessary to test this particular line of reasoning
more thoroughly, but as a concept it does provide for a

transitional period to full-scale farming from hunting-gathering, rather than a dramatic change.

Harvest of Emmer wheat.

One final point concerning Einkorn is its food value. With a protein level of over 17.5 per cent per gram dry weight it is an extremely attractive food source.

Emmer wheat, the result of a botanical accident involving the crossing of Einkorn and a wild goat grass, seems to have quickly supplanted Einkorn as the principal wheat of pre-history. Indeed, it was grown extensively throughout the Mediterranean area for many centuries, if not thousands of years and seeds of Emmer wheat were recovered from the pyramids in Egypt. It is said to have been grown as a main crop in Canada in this century.

At the Ancient Farm the major study is to evaluate the performance of Emmer wheat and other cereals, given all the variables involved. The programme envisaged is inevitably a long-term one and to date only the first phase has been completed. In order to evaluate any cereal performance it is necessary to do so over at least twenty successive seasons. At the end of that time, it should be possible to reach an average yield figure as well as a clear knowledge of maximum and minimum levels. In simple terms, we are trying to establish the probable yield figure that an Iron-Age farmer could reasonably expect. Thereafter, it may be possible to use such a figure in further calculations of numbers of hectares under cultivation and man-hours per crop and thus, perhaps, to postulate a population figure.

However, the process is not as simple as it first appears. The factors which affect cereal growth and yield are quite considerable; not least of these is the weather. Naturally there have been changes in the weather pattern over the last two thousand years, but the evidence, including that from pollen analysis, supports the view that there is a great similarity between the climate of Iron-Age and modern Britain. This is most convenient as it largely validates our results, but it is only a general statement. Within any climate there are small variations, all of which have a significant bearing on farming activity. The last three decades each demonstrate the different characteristics of long cold winters and dull summers, wet cool summers and fairly mild winters, hot summers and dry winters. Yet each variation can comfortably be absorbed into general statistical patterns.

Apart from the weather other variables are also significant, including the soil type, the use of manure, and crop rotation with nitrogen-users like wheat and nitrogen-fixers like beans. Any yield figure needs to be accompanied by a full description of the variables involved in its production. Thus, while the results of the first phase of the research programme at the Ancient Farm are of signal importance, they are only so in relation to the variables involved, and can only be applied to similar situations. The projected programme involves research plots set on all soil types and receiving exactly similar treatments.

However, the results so far achieved within the strict framework of the experimental programme based on Little Butser have been quite dramatic. As with Einkorn a major undertaking has been to increase the holding of seed while still asking specific questions of the cropping process. On a soil cover averaging ten centimetres thick over middle chalk, without any kind of fertilizer or any residual nutrient from previous land management, yield figures in excess of 2.5 tonnes to the hectare have been achieved while any average of 2 tonnes is not uncommon.

A further variable is, of course, the husbandry process itself. As discussed in chapter four, the ard was the major implement used in soil cultivation. From experiments with reconstructed ards carried out by the author, the tool has been shown to be extremely efficient on all soil types including heavy clay; in all cases it has left a furrow of over 15 cm deep. This is too deep for planting seed, so we must assume that a levelling process was carried out which produced a suitable tilth for a seed bed. How did the Iron-Age farmer sow his

A reconstruction of the Donnerupland Ard recovered from a peat bog in Denmark. In half a hectare of ploughing the unprotected oak share was worn down by 2.5 cm.

A sowing stick for drawing seed furrows in the tilth. For a successful crop it must be possible to hoe out the weeds.

seed ? The comfortable answer is that he broadcast the seed in the Roman fashion. However, while we have indications of many of his implements we have no evidence for a harrow, without which broadcasting seed is an extravagant way of feeding the birds.

I have elsewhere proposed the use of the 'sowing-stick' as a transitional implement from digging-stick to the ard and again suggest here that such a tool, a stick curved like an English hockey stick, may have been used to draw a shallow seed furrow. The advantages of this process are quite considerable. There is great control over the quantity of seed planted and the depth and position of planting, and it becomes possible to hoe the subsequent crop.

There is a wealth of ethnographic evidence from the temperate zones of Europe to support this proposition, although such parallels must be drawn with the greatest of care. Indeed, if we use this as a corroborative source, then a further alternative, that of dibbing the seed in small holes made with a dibbing-stick, must also be considered. However, by sowing-stick or dibbing-stick the end result is the same, the seed is safely planted and covered in rows. Both processes are used on the Farm in order not only to have a manageable crop, but also to be quite certain of the quantity of seed planted.

For both Emmer and Spelt one further variable is being examined, that of winter sowing as opposed to spring sowing, the seed source being the same. The number of experiments which need to be carried out are steadily increased by the questions raised by each completed phase. The research programme has hardly begun.

Another aspect of the research has been the recording of weed species which invade the growing crop. Because the Farm is protected against all modern sprays of fertilisers, herbicides and pesticides, the emergent weed species are of considerable interest. Today we are so accustomed to seeing cereal crops carefully marshalled with straw and heads all a standard height that we forget the appearance of fields as our grandparents knew them, infested with great quantities of other plants, many of which are now becoming extremely rare, if not already extinct. Consequently the Butser programme is helping in the conservation of such plants.

Einkorn, Emmer and Spelt are all bearded wheats and all are extremely difficult to thresh. It is easy to understand why they were superseded by easier threshing varieties, like Old Bread Wheat (*Triticum aestivum*) and Club Wheat (*Triticum compactum*). Yet there is much to be said for these early wheats especially with regard to their extremely high food value. The following table gives some indication of their relative merits to modern bread wheat.

Variety common name	Latin name	Protein value per cent (per gram dry weight)
Einkorn	Tr. monococcum	17.5
Emmer	Tr. dicoccum	20
Spelt	Tr. spelta	19
Bread Wheat (modern)	Tr. aestivum	8–9

Emmer wheat was the traditional bread wheat for the Roman army and its high protein value makes their achievement much more understandable. The only amino-acid missing from the chain is lycine, found abundantly in fish. Since the Romans were fond of a relish made from rotting fish guts, the perfect meal, directly comparable to the British fish and chips, was readily available.

Today Spelt wheat is grown in certain areas of Germany and the resultant bread is sold to the health-food market. They have overcome the threshing problem by putting the ears at least twice through the old-fashioned threshing drum before milling the flour.

One further discovery made from actually growing the crops and having to process them is the inefficiency of the so-called sickles of the Iron-Age period. In classical literature we read that the Celts only reaped the ear of the cereal. The problem is that, unlike modern varieties which have been selectively bred to a standard height, Emmer and Spelt grow like natural plants, fruiting at a number of levels often up to 75 cm apart on the same plant. It is no easy matter to grasp a handful of ears and deliver a neat cut with a sickle. On several tests with groups of volunteers, reconstructed sickles were tried and quickly discarded in favour of fingers. (This is a practice I recently observed in Spain where a family reaped a field, first picking off all the heads and putting them in baskets, and afterwards cutting the straw and tying it into bundles, or yealms.) The head breaks off easily enough at the rachis and the speed differential is remarkable. Also, the process does not disagree with the classical reference. However, it does leave a remarkable number of cutting objects at present called sickles. Although they are not particularly suited for the job, it does not necessarily mean they were not used for it. From their relative abundance at archaeological

sites they must represent a common tool and, if not a sickle, a plausible and very practical alternative is the spar-hook. This is a small, often crescent-shaped blade used for splitting hazel rods, willow withes and brambles. That this task was an extremely common one is supported not only by archaeological evidence, but also by our hard-earned experience from the research programme as a whole.

Apart from the cereals discussed above, it is extremely likely that a large number of other vegetable plants were grown. Again, we need to look carefully at the evidence offered by carbonised seeds. Almost immediately the sheer bulk of evidence is overwhelming. We must be consistent in our basic approach and examine their potential qualities and known histories as food plants before taking further steps. In the compass of this book it is impossible to take into account very many of these plants and the following varieties are cited simply because preliminary investigations concerning them have been undertaken at the Ancient Farm.

The best example of all is the Celtic bean (*Vicia faba minor*), which occurs fairly frequently in the lists of carbonised seeds. Not only is it a sound staple, but also it has a nitrogen nodule in its root system and consequently is ideal to rotate with a cereal crop. As such it forms part of a research programme which seeks to establish yield figures for spring-sown Emmer Wheat grown on ground which previously supported Celtic

A reconstructed sickle. There is a real practical doubt that such tools are sickles at all. It might have been a hook for splitting hazel rods.

The Celtic bean (*Vicia faba minor*).

beans. As a food they are nutritious and have a very pleasant nutty taste.

Within the same family the common vetch (*Vicia sativa*), which bears the blue flower, is also included among carbonised seeds. It provides edible fruits for man and a late herbage crop for animals.

Flax (*Linum usitatissimum*) was also grown and would have provided fodder from the leaves, linen obtained from the stalks by retting, and oil from the crushed seeds. The retting process also offers a further explanation for some of the huge pits commonly found on Iron-Age sites. Many pits are decidedly 'bath-shaped' and would have been ideal if lined with clay. For retting, the stalks of the flax plant are soaked in water for ten days or so to allow bacterial activity to break down the vegetable matter. Thereafter they are crushed, soaked for a further period and then combed out over spikes to extract the linen thread. Oil from the seeds would have had a large number of uses including cooking and lighting. A further plant may have been grown as a major crop for the supply of both edible and functional oil, gold of pleasure (*Calamina sativa*). This plant is now extremely rare although in the recent past it was quite common. It is strictly a native of the Mediterranean area but carbonised seeds have been recognised from the British Iron Age.

Many plants are, of course, weeds of cereal fields and it would be foolish to imagine them being specifically grown as main crops. Yet one needs to exercise great care, since many of them are edible and have been collected as food plants from time immemorial. Even the loathed charlock (*Sinapis arvensis*) is a member of the cabbage family and its new leaves are very palatable. A crop overtaken by it need not necessarily be viewed as a total disaster. The real loss is of a crop which can be effectively stored. A seasonal supply of greens is very useful, but does not keep for any appreciable length of time.

One particular plant, Fat Hen (*Chenopodium album*), turns up with increasing regularity in samples of carbonised seeds. Usually it has been regarded as a contaminant, appearing in a collection of seeds because it has inadvertently been harvested with the main crop. But, as stressed earlier in this chapter, carbonised seeds recovered by excavation are most unlikely to indicate either the function of a structure or agricultural practice. The most positive statement that can be made when a quantity of seeds of only one type is found is that it was either deliberately cultivated, most likely in the case of cereals, or deliberately collected from wild plants. Fat Hen is not only commonly found mixed in with other seeds, but has also been found hoarded in several excavations both in Northern Europe and the United Kingdom. Therefore, the second of our assumptions can be made, that the seed of Fat Hen may have been deliberately collected.

The cropping programme provided a further reason for the close consideration of Fat Hen. The spring-sown Emmer crop of 1973 ripened late, and because of continuous heavy rain in early September harvesting was delayed again and again. Finally, Fat Hen began to compete with the wheat, reaching the same height, or even exceeding it. Now it was possible simply by reaping the heads of the cereal, the process indicated by the documentary evidence, to gather by chance another seeding plant at the same time. However, it was easy to avoid this happening, so it cannot be used as an argument supporting the contamination of seed at the harvesting stage.

Fat Hen is a remarkable plant which has considerable food

value. Until the introduction of cabbage and spinach it is said to have been a main green vegetable in this country. Ironically it has a higher food value than either of its successors. Further, the seeds have been collected and ground into flour by a number of people, including certain tribes of North American Indians. Cattle and sheep find the leaves quite palatable and pigs consume it voraciously. In some areas it is called 'pig weed' or 'hog weed'. One other common name for Fat Hen is Melde and it is thought by this name to have contributed to place names like Maiden in Suffolk.

Its value and antiquity are well attested. How was it used in the Iron Age? At the minimum level, we can assume it was collected and eaten. Pure hoards of seed, on the other hand, may indicate that it was specifically grown as either a 'garden-type' vegetable or as a main crop. There are factors for and against the latter possibility. Fat Hen is extremely difficult to grow, since the seeds seem to be light conscious and like other weed seeds, many of the seeds lie dormant for some consider-able time and only a few germinate in any one year. This can be overcome agriculturally by over-sowing. The advantage of Fat Hen is its fairly short maturation period. If, for example, a cereal crop failed in the early part of the year, the field could be

Corn cockle (*Agrostemma Githago*), an arable weed. It is necessary to cultivate the right weeds to compete with the pre-historic cereals. Many weeds are now virtually extinct.

sown with Fat Hen and a valuable crop obtained within three-and-a-half months, say June to September. Thus there would be late fodder for the cattle, sheep and goats into mid-autumn and seed for grinding into flour. The study of Fat Hen is being undertaken not only at the Ancient Farm but also at other agricultural research centres seeking alternative protein sources from green plants.

Finally in this brief chapter on crops and plants, it is worth mentioning yet another unpopular plant, Black Bindweed (*Convolvulus arvensis*), a weed of crops and waste ground. Carbonised seed of this plant has also been recovered from excavations indicating that it may have been deliberately collected. The seeds, triangular in section, are similar in appearance to Buck wheat (*Fagopyrum esculentum*) and can be ground up into flour to make a very acceptable bread.

Yet, despite the above arguments and hypotheses, the opposite case needs to be put to re-establish a simple perspective. Apart from the cereals for which there is a clear case in support of cultivation, the vast majority of other carbonised seeds could well be the result of bonfires built to burn the weeds gathered from the fields at the end of the harvest.

A grain storage pit; the grain skin averages 2–3 cm thick.

6 *The Pit*

In the majority of Iron Age sites which have been excavated, the pit is the most important piece of archaeological evidence. This is especially true on chalklands, sand and gravels, and to a lesser extent on limestone areas. The pits come in varying shapes and sizes, from just a few centimetres to over three metres deep. The Iron Age, more than any other period, is typified by these features. For many of the pits we have no sound interpretation to offer, and a greater understanding of their purpose would be the key to a better knowledge of the Iron Age as a whole. Of course there are many suggestions for pit usage and function, but the state of present knowledge is still very slight. Much of the research programme of the Butser Ancient Farm has therefore been devoted to experimenting with pits.

One of the greatest difficulties of pit archaeology is that the excavator is faced with the final function of a pit which has little or no connection with its original or even secondary purpose. Pits are often described in reports as 'rubbish pits'. Precisely what this means is often difficult to understand when the term rubbish is analysed. In a society which operates on an agricultural economy, apart from fragments of pottery and occasional metal objects which have cheated chemical breakdown by their nature or by chance position, all the rubbish is organic and therefore decomposes. Further, since we believe that the manuring of fields took place, organic rubbish was, in all probability, deposited in the midden and ultimately spread on the fields. 'Rubbish' is therefore an inaccurate description.

The majority of pits have been deliberately back-filled, either at one time or over a number of occasions, with rubble obtained for the purpose, or else they have steadily silted up. Even this last suggestion is open to some debate, since one wonders from where the silt actually comes. When a pit is dug, especially into chalk (although the same argument applies for sand and limestone), a large amount of material is thrown up. The result is a hole for a specific function and a large pile of unwanted material, which represents a considerable hazard. For chalk, one means of disposal is to spread it onto the fields as a dressing material, a farming practice carried out until quite recently in southern England, where many chalk or marl pits are to be found. Alternatively, the material gained can be used in banks or roadways, in house construction or even to fill

A cylindrical storage pit cut into the chalk rock. The smoothing of the rock walls is caused by the germinating 'grain skin' during storage.

up other pits whose prime function has now been completed. In effect, unless we imagine settlement areas to have been dotted with piles of rubble placed immediately adjacent to the open mouths of pits, it is difficult to see how any natural silting process can have happened. One extremely simple experiment carried out at the Farm was designed to test the silting hypothesis. In three years not one lump of chalk rubble fell from a pile placed twenty centimetres away from the mouth of the pit. In fact, the only silting that took place was occasioned by rabbits and mice, and rabbits, as mentioned earlier, were not to be found in prehistoric Britain.

Nonetheless, much can be learned from excavating a pit, especially if the excavation is total and taken out layer by layer. There is no place for the pick and shovel among the equipment for such an excavation. For a pit that has been deliberately back-filled, it is not impossible to work out from which side or sides the shovelling took place. Again, much artefactual evidence has been discovered in pits, and it is possible by comparing collections of material from different pits not only to consider the chronology of the material according to its position in the layers, but also to identify pits of the same period. It is also from the contents of pits that the majority of carbonised seeds have been recovered. The

Some pits may have been lined with basketwork.

contents are indeed most important, but it must be stressed again that they are frequently totally divorced from the original function of the pit.

To investigate the function of a pit, we need to consider it as a purpose-built subterranean structure. Minute examination and recording of pit walls is therefore of prime importance, as it would be for a building above ground. In order to make progress in our understanding and appreciation of these underground structures, experimental research is both fundamental and extremely urgent. An instrument devised specifically for pit excavation, but which has much wider applications, is described in detail in the following chapter. It represents one of the positive contributions to have been made in this field to date.

The main purpose in this chapter, however, is to explain how the pit may have been used in the one area of food storage and the principal line of enquiry has been into the storage of grain underground. A classical reference suggests that pits were used to store foodstuffs, especially grain, but it would be wrong to assume that all pits were used in this way. Some alternative interpretations are discussed later.

Storing grain in underground silos has been quite common practice in many parts of the world in different periods of

time. Today, for example, there is provision in South America
for underground storage of over two million tonnes of grain.
Many African tribes stored their grain in pits similar in scale
to those of the Iron Age and North American Indians
followed the same practice. But for each individual case there
are variables which make direct comparisons most difficult to
draw. The majority of instances quoted above all involve grain
dried to at least ten per cent moisture content before storage.
In the Roman period, when they stored grain in overhead
granaries, there is an abundance of evidence for grain-drying
floors and kilns, but for the Iron Age no such provision has
been found.

What happens, therefore, when grain is stored without
being dried to a low moisture content, but just as it is when
reaped from the fields? The process is fairly simple. Grain,
like human beings, uses up oxygen and gives off carbon
dioxide in its normal respiration cycle. When placed in a
sealed container the grain initially uses all the oxygen present
and produces an atmosphere loaded with carbon dioxide. At
this point it enters a state of unstable dormancy. The
instability is caused by the presence of micro-organisms,
fungi and bacteria, which were present in the field and go into
the container with the grain. Depending upon the temperature within the container and its impermeability, these micro-
organisms will be either active or inactive. If the former, then
deterioration of the grain will be fairly rapid with a real
possibility of its becoming toxic.

Grain is normally reaped from the field at about 16 per cent
moisture content. Ideally every farmer prefers it to be lower,
but 16 per cent is a good average. In modern circumstances it
is normally dried to approximately 13–12 per cent. The
modern storage system, however, depends upon air flow
through and around the grain.

At the Farm a number of pits were excavated to replicate
the Iron-Age ones generally thought to have been storage pits.
In broad terms there are two basic shapes, the cylinder and the
beehive. Both have an average capacity in excess of one tonne
of threshed grain. The purpose of the experimental programme is to examine exactly what happens inside a storage
pit and to compare the effects on storage of different pit shapes
and types of lining material. There is some suggestion in the
archaeological record for clay-lined and basket-lined pits.
The normal storage period spans the winter months, since the
activity of fungi and bacteria is inhibited by low temperature
patterns. Before and after storage comprehensive tests are

made of the germination quality of the grain as well as its moisture content.

The physical process is as follows: the grain is poured directly into a pit cut into surface chalk rock flush with the ground (sand and gravel or limestone pits work equally well); gas aspiration tubes for sampling purposes and bead thermistors are inserted at relevant points within the grain body; the pit is sealed with a plug of clay plastered directly onto the surface of the grain and extended for a further twenty centimetres beyond the edges of the pit (some African tribes use dung for this purpose, as Iron-Age man may have done); an earth cap is put onto the clay seal to keep it moist, so inhibiting the passage of rain water or oxygen into the pit. Immediately after sealing, the grain directly under the clay plug begins to increase its respiration cycle because of the presence of moisture. The resultant waste product, carbon dioxide, being heavier than the intergranular atmosphere, sinks down into the rest of the pit and so inhibits any further respiration in the stored mass of grain.

The interim results of this necessarily long-term experiment are quite dramatic. Grain can be stored in the above manner at sixteen per cent moisture content most successfully. The loss in germination is normally minimal and usually less than in most modern systems; the physical loss in an unlined pit is approximately two per cent of the stored

For the research experiments, instruments to measure temperature and gas concentration are inserted into the pit when it is filled.

mass. The prerequisites for successful storage are a low temperature during the storage period, an impermeable seal, a good production of carbon dioxide and, finally, a subsoil which naturally inhibits lateral water flow.

The implications, even at this stage, are critically important. Contrary to accepted theories, it is not necessary to parch the grain before storage. Not only is there a distinct lack of archaeological evidence for parching the grain, but also it is counterproductive to do so, because the stored mass would be likely to attract moisture. More important, grain stored in this way has a high germination quality and could well be thought of as seed grain and not consumption grain. The argument for population estimations based upon pit capacity and *per capita* consumption cannot now be logically applied. In addition, there is no evidence forthcoming from some consecutive years of pit usage to support the principle that a pit becomes musty or contaminated in some way to prohibit its further use. Pits can be used again and again without any apparent reason for their abandonment. Should a pit go wrong, the reasons for storage failure cannot be attributed to the pit itself. The only reason for pit failure other than bad sealing or rodent infestation is excessive rainfall, which causes lateral flow instead of vertical flow, thus allowing water penetration at underground levels.

Apart from ritual reasons which we shall never be able to establish by excavation, the only possible cause for abandoning a pit is the farmer's reaction to failure. When the stored grain is affected by water, the effects are remarkable. The fungal and bacterial infestation can cause strange and weird colourations, such as shiny reds, dull browns and violent greens. Faced with such a prospect, which is not enhanced by the accompanying ill odour, no farmer could be blamed for digging a new pit and abandoning the old to the evil spirits. Yet there is nothing wrong at all with the pit itself, only with the stored grain. One experiment in operation at present is to reproduce these evil conditions and then abandon the pit, but monitor its disintegration. Ultimately, the grain should rot down to nothing more than a thin black layer. Such layers have been recorded but never analysed.

In effect, the experimental programme has so far established a number of clear facts which demand revised interpretations for this particular area. One further observation that requires emphasis is the physical capacity of these pits. If indeed they are grain storage pits and if their capacity is over a tonne of grain, consider the amount of land that must inevitably have been under cultivation. From the crop programme, taking only the best yield figures available, a minimum of three to four Celtic fields were required to fill one pit. On average figures between five and six Celtic fields were needed. (The average area of a Celtic field is about 0.13 hectares.) On a large number of sites there are literally hundreds of pits of suitable shape and size to qualify as grain storage pits, and even with only a very small percentage in contemporary use, a great area of land must have been in cultivation. If we revert to the standard but unacceptable theories of low yield (around half a tonne to the hectare), then it is necessary to multiply by four the above estimations of fields required to fill a pit. In either case, the major implication is that in the Iron Age there was virtually total domination of the landscape and a proportionately large population. This implication has been supported and enhanced recently by aerial photography. The landscape, especially of southern England, is now shown to be covered by undreamt-of numbers of sites shown by parch and crop marks in the unusual drought conditions of 1976. It will be several years before the aerial survey work carried out during this remarkable season is finally processed. The initial results, however, suggest that our problem in the future will be to isolate the areas where prehistoric man was not active.

There are many products other than grain which can be stored in pits. It is very useful to experiment with them all in order to discover exactly how well various foods store, and more significantly what physical imprint the storage process may leave on the sides of a pit. It is this imprint which may allow us to ascribe potential function to pits excavated on Iron-Age sites and, indeed, sites of other periods, particularly the Neolithic. The experiments are not quite as simple as the above statement may suggest because there are great technical difficulties in recording evidence, not only for the test pits to use for comparative purposes, but also in recording such detail from excavated pits. For example, preliminary trials have been carried out with photographic recording, utilising wide-angle lenses. The ideal system would employ a fish-eye lens, but the cost is quite prohibitive for the research programme and certainly for the normal excavation budget. A system of a mosaic of colour photographs is the present state of achievement. Apart from visual records there is a growing realisation of the need for chemical analysis of the outermost layer of the wall structure of a pit, especially at those levels where immediate sealing after usage may have taken place.

For example, one simple function of a pit is for the salting of meats of various types. Salting meat is a practice which has an incredibly long tradition which could easily predate the Iron Age. The question raised by the hypothesis is the potential chemical residues that may have been locked inside the pit. Salt is extremely soluble but uncommon in the general geology and, if isolated in an archaeological feature, it would indicate a deliberate human activity. There are a number of salt production sites of this period already isolated along the eastern and southern coasts of England and presumably there are more to be discovered. Although there is some debate about man's actual need for salt, we can reasonably assume that it was an important commodity and that it may even have been imported. If it was used for meat preservation inside the typical storage type pit, then great quantities of salt were necessary. Estimating very widely that at least eighty per cent of the storage space would be occupied by meat, for a pit with a capacity of a cubic metre, at least twenty kilograms of salt would have to be used to ensure a successful process. The hypothesis is sound enough; what is needed now is the recognition of the hypothesis by excavators and the subsequent collection of pit wall samples for analysis.

A second probability that may prove easier to verify is the manufacture of silage. In a mixed agricultural economy the maintenance of livestock through the winter is of paramount importance. The essence of farming is to acquire sufficient food during the growing seasons to maintain both humans and animals through the winter. Fortunately, the old idea of wholesale slaughter of animals each autumn has receded, since were it to be practised consistently no animal would reach maturity. Inevitably autumn is the time to cull herds and flocks but there is a significant difference between selective slaughter and wholesale butchery. Contrary to the accepted belief that silage-making is a relatively modern activity, there is clear evidence that it is a very old practice indeed. In the north of Scotland and the Hebrides there is a tradition of making winter fodder from grass, even flowered grass, in small sealed pits. Making silage is dependent upon the activity of a bacterium, found naturally on grass, which manufactures a liquid called lactic acid. This bacterial activity takes place when wilted grass is gathered into a container, for example a pit, and sealed off. The lactic acid, which has a pervasive sickly sweet smell, acts as a preservative or pickling agent to the grass in an exactly similar way as vinegar preserves onions. If the silage is made in a pit cut into chalk rock, the acid will react with the chalk and produce a deposit called calcium lactate. This substance, slightly less soluble than salt, could be sealed inside a pit which has been immediately back-filled after use, and so identified by excavators.

It is obviously, therefore, necessary in excavation practice not only to extract the fill or contents of a pit, but also to record in detail the wall structure and to take samples for chemical analysis. Even if the analyses prove to be negative, the information is still of positive value.

Apart from salting and silage it is possible to store a variety of other foods in the same way as grain. Ethnography shows us that it is not at all uncommon. The North American Indians stored a variety of food in underground pits both inside and outside their houses. In Switzerland even green vegetables were stored in sealed underground pits. If we consider the evidence from carbonised seeds we can suggest that Celtic beans could have been kept in this way. Hazel nuts and beech mast are further possibilities.

Of course, not all pits would have been used for food storage. There are a number of sound and necessary alternatives, some of which could also be identified by chemical analysis. Water storage is an obvious candidate. A pit lined with clay (and there is considerable evidence to support clay linings), would make an adequate subterranean water butt. Since the Iron Age possessed the technology of stave construction, however, there may have been barrels or butts for this purpose. Much is made of the problems of water supply in the prehistoric period, especially on the southern chalkdowns. There are two basic factors to consider. First, we have lowered the general water table by some 60 m in the last thirty years by our increased demand for industry and personal hygiene. Second, the natural spring line would have issued at the interface between the supposed loess deposit, which has now been eroded away, and the capping of clay-with-flints, common along much of the downs. It is not inconceivable that from a number of settlements the collection of water may have meant an uphill walk to start with. On others the water supply may have been within the settlement itself.

Pits may also have been used in the leather tanning process, the results of which might well lead to confusion of identification between a latrine and a tanning pit in that urine was common to both. Further, dyeing may also have been a 'pit activity'. The manufacture of woad dye is not a dissimilar process from that of indigo, for which the Africans use pits.

Potters, too, had a use for the pit. Several pits have been

A raised platform supported by four posts for a haystack. The stack is built around the central pole.

excavated which have been full of washed clay, and are thought to be for the maturing of the clay prior to its manufacture into pots. Other pits have been discovered to contain quantities of 'sling stones' and perhaps represent arsenals, though this would be hardly a system of rapid armament in a time of crisis.

Finally, there are a large number of ritual shafts. These lie outside the scope of this book but it is interesting to muse upon the possibility that the ritual shaft might be a secondary phase of a functional pit. A grain storage pit which failed at a particularly difficult time might easily be turned into a propitiatory device for the gods.

In considering the storage of food, we must take into account other structures that are indicated by post-hole patterns. On many excavations rectangular structures are proposed about two by three metres, based upon the regular arrangements of four and five post-holes. These are usually interpreted as granaries, on the basis of evidence drawn from ethnography. The normal inference is a platform, supported by four posts, which carries a large clay or daub container shaped like a huge storage jar. The open top is normally covered with a removable thatched roof, which also protects the walls of the pot itself. If, on the other hand, one is considering a simple wooden shed set on piles comparable to staddle stones and filled with loose grain, it is as well to remember that loose grain exerts two-thirds of its weight in lateral pressure. With a potential capacity of twelve cubic metres, the walls would need to withstand a thrust of approximately eight tonnes. It would have to be a very stout shed indeed.

Although there may be some justification in this explanation, there are a number of equally valid possibilities. It is a major function of the Ancient Farm Project to examine the relationships of the various processes and activities that are vital to the operation of a farming unit, and it soon became clear that four-post structures could serve a multitude of functions, some more important than granaries. Interpretation of four-post structures is particularly difficult because, unlike a round-house with a limited number of variables, rectangular buildings can be built in so many ways that no reconstruction can have a high degree of authority.

Chief among the possible functions of four-post structures are barns, byres, sheds for waggons or carts, chicken houses and stables. It has even been suggested that they might be houses though, with the presence of spacious round-houses, a dwelling no larger than a modern garden shed is difficult to

This type of haystack was once a common sight in many parts of England. When protected with a thatch cover hay can be stored for long periods in this way.

accept. One reconstruction of a simple barn based upon four post-holes was built by the author some years ago. Its purpose was to demonstrate the great difficulty posed by these configurations and the multiplicity of choice they offer. When its capacity was calculated, it was found by coincidence to equal the straw bulk of Emmer wheat from a hundred square metres. The example is worth citing simply because it is so easy to be attracted to and persuaded by coincidence. There is always the need for consistent replication of results before an hypothesis may be tentatively accepted as valid.

Structures for the storage of hay are another possible interpretation of the post-hole evidence. One traditional system in this and other temperate countries is to build a haystack around a central pole (which gives yet a further possible interpretation of the solitary post-hole as discussed in chapter three). Because of sloping ground at the farm it was found necessary to build a horizontal raft to support a haystack, and this offers a very workmanlike interpretation of a five-post structure and is in fact based directly upon archaeological evidence.

7 Data Recovery

Experimental archaeology in all its forms depends entirely upon the basic data provided by excavation and to a much lesser extent on such documentary evidence as may be extant. This data has consistently proved to be inadequate in building such a complex and all-embracing project as the Ancient Farm, where the most searching questions are asked of it. Perhaps the evidence is either not there to be recovered or else our present systems of recovery are too crude to recognise its presence. Many of the great generalisations which provide the literature of prehistory, while valuable and even potentially correct, are founded upon untested and unproven guesswork. The hypothesised 'fact' is unfortunately a commonplace one in archaeological reasoning.

If experimental archaeology can improve the recognition and evaluation of the evidence, it has made a fundamental contribution to the progress of archaeology as a whole. Consequently it is one of the aims of the Research Project not only to feed back into the process of field archaeology alternative interpretations and a facility for the physical testing of hypotheses, but also to suggest new systems of data recovery and recording which may be of significant value. There is little point in just underlining the inadequacy of archaeological data, since this is already appreciated by most archaeologists. Such criticism as comes from the Ancient Farm is designed specifically to be constructive. The purpose of this chapter, therefore, is to outline four experiments which are in process at present to seek improved data recovery and recording, and to provide data modules for comparative purposes.

The standard practice when beginning a rural excavation is to remove the turf, since the evidence is to be found below it. In these days of urgent rescue excavations it is common to see this work executed by a bulldozer or similar earthmoving equipment. In fact, there is a handbook on such machines produced specifically for the archaeologist! Yet amongst archaeologists, both professional and amateur, the belief is widely held that the majority of evidence from a site is to be found on the spoil heap.

In ordinary fieldwork many sites have been located by the discovery of potsherds and other artefacts in the plough-soil, clearly turned up by the plough during cultivation. Invariably these concentrations of material lie over the site unless there is an appreciable slope involved. In the latter case there is often a soil flow down the slope which also carries downhill the archaeological remains. From aerial photography we know of many sites which are isolated by no other means than soil marks.

These considerations, very briefly outlined, served as the inspiration for the following experiment. It seemed reasonable to consider possible ways of excavating a site from the grass surface downwards. This is especially necessary on the chalklands of southern England where ten centimetres of soil cover is not uncommon. Thereafter, of course, one is in the comparative safety of rock-cut features.

The grass itself is the greatest enemy to be defeated. The life-cycle of any green plant depends upon the conversion of sunlight into energy, a process called photosynthesis. To effect its removal it is necessary to interrupt this process, but in such a way as not to damage the soil structure or its inhabitants. A herbicide is not the answer, especially since many excavations of rural sites are on prime farmland.

The method adopted was simply to exclude the sunlight. A layer of opaque black plastic sheeting, the kind used to cover silage pits, was laid over an area of grass and carefully pegged down with wooden battens and wire pegs. The total area covered for the experiment was exactly one hundred square metres. The location for the trial was part of the Little Butser Spur, where there were ephemeral signs of prehistoric occupation. As indicated previously, the soil cover on Little Butser averages just over ten centimetres.

Great care was taken during the trial period to ensure that rain water could flow under the plastic sheet and thus admit oxygen to the creatures in the soil. It was of paramount importance not to produce a barren patch on the research area. The trial itself took place during the spring months although the timing is critical only in so far as the grass must be growing.

Checks were carried out at weekly intervals, and after six weeks, enough grass had been killed to admit crude trowel work. This factor alone led to the immediate refinement of the standard trowel used in excavation. All the alternate working edges of the diamond-shaped trowel blade were filed sharp. In this way it was possible to cut carefully through the dead and dying rootstock. The sharpening of alternate edges of the trowel blade allowed its use by both right and left handed workers, and also each individual could select one of two cutting edges and thus rest but still use his wrist.

After twelve weeks the experiment proved totally successful. A grass cover was quite defeated and it was possible to lift off the dead vegetation including the roots. The fascinating by-product of the experiment was the discovery of a distribution of Iron Age potsherds on the surface of the now bare plot. In effect, they had been held in suspension by the grass roots. The experiment released these root-bonded sherds in position. The soil, too, was in an ideal state for visual examination and for excavation. It was possible, for example, to observe concentrations of chalk granules which indicated an archaeological feature. Furthermore, it was possible to survey the area exactly without the variables of vegetation cover.

Clear conclusions may be drawn from this experiment. In a rural area, where even rescue digs have regularly twelve weeks' notice before excavation need begin, it would be possible to excavate literally from the grass surface downwards, recording soil anomalies, sherd and artefact distributions and observing any correlation between these findings and the rock-cut features beneath. For a research excavation today the use of an earthmoving machine is almost unthinkable.

A final postscript to this experiment is the ever-present need to continue the investigations, begun in the last century by Charles Darwin, into the activities of the earthworm. Worm-counts are regularly carried out at the Ancient Farm to establish any changes brought about by different field and grassland treatments. As Darwin pointed out, certain varieties of earthworm can effectively invert the soil cover over a period of years. In so doing, surface material like pieces of broken pot can be transferred to a considerable depth. Several long-term experiments are at present in hand to furnish further information on this process. However, with only ten centimetres of soil cover such worm activity seems to have been negated by root growth.

A second major experiment which is at present undergoing preliminary field trials is a direct result of the previous one. On a number of research excavations in recent years serious attempts have been made to plot the exact field position, horizontal and vertical, of every artefact as it is recovered. Initially, the purpose has been to establish the presence or otherwise of any patterns of deposition. In chapter three I suggested the possibility of artefact patterns indicating the position of the walls of houses made of turf or cob. Extending that argument further there is no reason why such patterns, if they exist at all, should not indicate the occupation pattern of a settlement. A further theory has been proposed that successive occupation layers, not shown by structural changes, may be traced by the precise plotting and categorising of artefacts in their vertical stratification within a building.

There would seem to be a clear case for a practical experiment to test whether such theories, and the enormous amount of painstaking work they involve, are actually sensible in terms of adequate return. The greatest disturbing agency in the countryside, beyond the activity of the earthworm, is the impact of ploughing and cultivation generally. That plough damage occurs is beyond question, and examples can be readily cited of ploughed-out barrows, villas, walls – the list is without end. However, we are not yet sure of the extent to which ploughing will move small artefacts like sherds of pottery. Many sites are beneath plough depth, yet their presence has been attested by concentrations of sherds and, quite often, nothing else. Presumably, therefore, if the sherds are employed as indicators, then they cannot have been moved far. Allowing that movement has taken place, has it been enough to disturb beyond recall the original deposition pattern, should one have existed?

With these questions in mind, the following field trial has been designed as a preliminary exercise. Ultimately, if the field trial proves to have positive results, it is planned to operate a full-scale programme in as many areas and soil types as possible.

A fairly flat area of a hundred square metres has been selected on the high downs in Hampshire in the middle of a large field. The selection was quite deliberate in order to avoid unusual activity on the field boundaries. On cereal fields, for example, the edges are often ploughed prior to stubble burning. The purpose has been to find an area which will be subjected to all forms of normal agricultural activity as required within the next five years' life of the field. The area has been surveyed to fifty-centimetre centres and keyed in to a fixed surveyor's bench-mark. Thereafter, according to the precise grid pattern artificial sherds have been planted exactly thirty centimetres below the ground surface at each intersection of the grid.

The construction of the artificial sherd presented considerable problems. It needed to be strong, yet of comparative weight and shape to a sherd of prehistoric pottery, and it had to be easy to find again. After a number of trials, which included the use of radioactive material and Geiger counters, the final result consists of a diamond-shaped resin sherd containing a small stick magnet and a number. This sherd can be readily located with a fluxgate gradiometer or magneto-meter. The trial area was, of course, previously swept with the gradiometer to avoid unnecessary complications.

Subsequent phases of the trial consist simply in resurveying the plot and locating and recording the spatial position of each numbered sherd after every agricultural operation which physically moves the soil about. In due course, and after each known operation, we will obtain a 'history' for each sherd and its spatial relationship with immediately adjacent sherds. Once a sufficient body of data has been built up it will be possible, probably with computer help, to impose questions of pattern and subsequent pattern distortions. In fig. 2 I have indicated three basic patterns that can be imposed on the original grid design and whose subsequent histories can be plotted. Only those sherds which occur within each hatched area will be significant for that area. Immediately it can be seen that a sherd is not exclusive to one pattern and that within the design the same pattern can be imposed a number of times using different sherds. The results will be most interesting and potentially very significant.

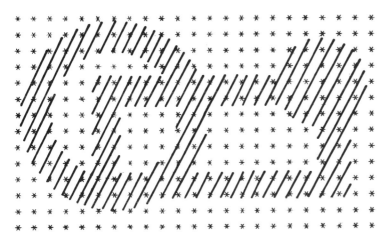

Fig. 2 The basic grid in the initial phase of the experi-ment; * represents an artificial sherd; the hatched areas represent possible positions of structures.

One major difficulty, especially in reconstruction work, is the lack of precise recorded measurements from excavations. For many years, for example, it was considered quite adequate to record a post-hole as a black blob on a plan with no further information given concerning its precise shape, depth, general capacity, presence or absence of packing material or the nature of its side walls. The emphasis was exclusively upon patterns. Fortunately there is a change in practice and details

of such features which are, in fact, extremely complex are more regularly being given. However, such is the present convention that only a section drawing is provided. This, too, is really inadequate unless the post-hole is quite uniform. It is not only for reconstruction purposes that a full-scale volumetric record is required, but also for any analysis and appraisal of a site. What is true of post-holes is also inevitably true of pits, gulleys or any other feature.

To make a post-hole is a most educational experience, especially if a post is actually put into it. Rapidly one learns that there are a multiplicity of post-hole types. Physical construction varies considerably depending on the nature of the post and its expected function. For example, a fence post is often driven into the ground into a previously made hole. This, in turn, is made with an iron bar or heavy wooden pole tipped with a metal or stone spike. A handaxe makes a splendid tip for such a bar. The hole made in this way is always slightly smaller than the post for which it is intended. The post thereafter is driven into place with a heavy baulk of timber or perhaps a beetle, the old-fashioned one-piece wooden mallet usually fashioned from a fallen yew tree. Inevitably the hole is altered in shape but traces of the bar

A fence of upright stakes with interwoven hazel rods. Fences like this are still to be found in many poor areas especially in Northern Ireland.

activity can usually be located at the bottom. The shape of this kind of hole is different from that made by a post which is simply driven into the ground. In both cases the posts, while initially firm and integral to the fence structure, are ultimately supported by the fence itself. Should the fence be further subjected to pressure of any kind, the post-hole will also be altered in form. Indeed, it is possible from a line of fence post-holes, where the fence has been a substantial one, to determine the direction of a prevailing wind.

This is not the place for a treatise upon the differing natures of post-holes. It is enough to state that they are many and various and that it is necessary archaeologically to describe in detail post-holes found during excavation. Our concern here is in the method of recording post-holes and pits in adequate and precise detail. It is both impractical and too expensive to expect multiple section drawings in excavation reports but it is reasonable to expect a numerical analysis of such features. It is to this end that the 'protophit' was designed.

The protophit is a simple measuring device consisting of an horizontal bar which can be levelled into the site exactly using spirit levels built into the tool. Along the bar is fixed a

The protophit: a simple device for accurate measurement of archaeological features.

travelling chuck which supports a vertical and movable rod. Both horizontal bar and vertical rod (there are two supplied, a small 'fine tuner' and a large one some two metres in length) are graduated in centimetres with measurement points located in the chuck. The main horizontal bar is made of polished steel, while all the other parts are made of aluminium. The legs which support the horizontal bar are infinitely adjustable being fitted with a universal joint and locking nut. The whole apparatus can be dismantled and carried in a standard saloon car.

The advantages offered by this tool are a considerable advance on the sagging string line so often employed as a datum, as it offers a means of producing in numerical form a three-dimensional record of any feature. A further attachment has been designed to cope with undercut features. All measurements can be taken to an accuracy of two millimetres.

The following example, which describes an emptied feature, demonstrates the number of sections which can be achieved numerically. The figures are recorded across a square plan at two centimetre intervals, the protophit being moved across a straight base line set east-west. The figure o signifies the ground datum level – all other figures in the table are below the datum line. No less than twenty-two standard sections can be drawn on north-south and east-west axes as well as a number of diagonal sections. Likewise areas of a similar depth can be easily seen. In effect the table of figures

	1	2	3	4	5	6	7	8	9	10	11	12	
1	o	o	o	o	o	3	o	1	1	2	2	3	
2	o	o	o	o	5	10	7	3	1	2	2	2	
3	o	o	o	5	10	12	10	5	2	3	3	2	
4	o	o	10	12.5	15	17	24	30	29	26	26	1	
5	o	5	9	15	17	20	21	26	30	31	32	1	
6	o	5	7	14	19	21	24	27	32	30	30	2	
7	o	o	5	12	17	20	20	25	30	29	28	2	
8	o	o	4	10	16	21	23	27	29	28	28	3	NORTH
9	o	o	o	7	15	17	19	22	24	26	3	3	
10	o	o	o	o	6	12	16	18	22	3	4	4	
11	o	o	o	o	o	3	9	16	3	3	3	4	
12	o	o	o	o	o	o	7	12	2	3	3	3	
13	o	o	o	o	o	o	o	o	2	3	3	3	

BASE
LINE

gives a total appreciation of the feature which is a shallow stake hole from which the rotted stake had been levered and wrenched free.

Such a numerical analysis is easily stored on prepared cards and with a little explanation could be used for publication. Even the measurements taken on site are made easier. Since no drawing is involved, the figures can be read directly into a tape recorder. The same process holds true for the recording of different layers and objects within a feature, and if necessary both precise plans and sections can be drawn after the excavation. Although such a tool is extremely flexible it will only be as accurate as the operator and, more to the point, will only record the skill of the excavator.

The final section of this chapter is devoted to an entirely different kind of experiment, but nonetheless one designed to aid the excavator in the field. So far I have discussed the physical aids to excavation that may come from the experiment utilising black plastic, the interpretative potential of sherd distribution and a new measuring device. Many of the experiments carried out at the Farm start from the hypothesis position only: because Iron-Age farmers did this, then they must have been able to do that, although as yet we have no clear evidence of it. One particular example is the production of charcoal. It is necessary fuel within the domestic economy for the Iron Age but, more importantly, it is vital for smelting and heating metal.

The traditional 'how' of charcoal production is relatively well known. Indeed there are charcoal burners alive today from whom one can still obtain detailed information. Ironically, charcoal burners in the New Forest area even built small thatched round-houses in which they lived during the working season. Archaeologically, the remains of such houses would undoubtedly be confusing.

Charcoal is produced by burning timber in an earth and turf-covered clamp in such a way that only a minimum amount of oxygen reaches the fire, the combustion depending for the greatest part on the natural gases in the wood. Today, charcoal is manufactured by heating sealed metal vats filled with timber.

However, we assume that the traditional method is the one typical of the Iron-Age period because there are virtually no other alternatives. Since, to my knowledge, no evidence of charcoal-burning areas has been isolated for the Iron Age, it seems necessary to provide comparative evidence to aid such isolation. We need to know, therefore, what kind of evidence is made by a charcoal clamp that could be discovered archaeologically. The answer to this question is being sought by repeatedly manufacturing charcoal in the same clamp area. The primary phase of this operation was to excavate the area and record in great detail the underlying chalk rock. The topsoil was then replaced and compacted before building the first clamp. During the firing of all the clamps no abnormal care is taken beyond that necessary for good charcoal production. Subsequent examinations of the clamp foundation are scheduled after the first and every successive fifth clamp. To date the first and fifth have been examined.

The result of the first clamp indicated only a breakdown in the soil cover and a general admixture of charcoal fragments. After the fifth clamp, however, there was a significant breakdown of the underlying chalk surface with the beginning of a distinct hollow. In due course it should be possible to establish what kind of evidence the process does leave behind and so offer it as a standard for comparison, a *comparandum* for the field archaeologist. The basic and correct criticism of this particular experiment is the assumption that more than one clamp was burned in the same place. There is traditional evidence from the charcoal burners which is in favour of repeated burnings in the same place over a period of months and occasionally for a year or more, and therefore it seems reasonable to pursue this course. Indeed, the initial findings, although too early to be more than tentative, suggest a possible interpretation for the so-called 'working hollow'.

Throughout this chapter I have attempted to outline positive contributions that experiment can offer to archaeology, and to underline its fundamental role within the subject. Experiment is concerned with focusing attention onto the minutiae. If these are unsatisfactory, then it is only sensible that this should be recognised, and that further experiments be designed to improve the situation.

8 *Laboratory to Living Museum*

As the Ancient Farm slowly took shape on Little Butser, its popularity grew. From the very beginning the concept captured the imagination of both professionals and laymen. Television and radio have shown continued interest and there has been an annual programme of over one hundred public lectures. Organisations in Denmark, France, Germany and the United States of America have figured on the lecture and conference circuit. But all this interest could not be contained within lecture theatre and seminar room. More and more parties wanted to visit the site, to see for themselves the experiments, the houses, the crops, which were fundamentally revising the old accepted theories. This pressure became so severe that there was a distinct risk that it would introduce a further and unacceptable variable to the experimental work.

Consequently, when in late 1975 the Hampshire County Council offered to the project a further two-hectare site adjacent to the new Queen Elizabeth Park Centre to develop

The Pimperne house dressed for a television film.

as a demonstration area, we eagerly accepted. A demonstration area would not only relieve the pressure on the research site but also would provide, in due course, adequate funding to maintain both itself and the expanding research programme. Little thought was given at the time to the personnel involved since no immediate increase in staff was contemplated. Perhaps the great drought of 1976, so disastrous in prehistoric farming terms, proved to be a blessing in disguise because it allowed a concentrated effort to be made on the construction of the demonstration area. The heat was so intense that the normal hoeing programme, an absorber of a great many man-hours in the early part of the year, had to be abandoned. Similarly, haymaking was a non-event simply because the grass failed to grow. The time saved was put to good use.

The intention was to build into the demonstration area representations of all the experimental work carried out on the research site. The challenge was both daunting and stimulating. In effect, the end product had to become a living

View of the excavated site at Pimperne, Dorset. (Photo courtesy of Prof. D. W. Harding.)

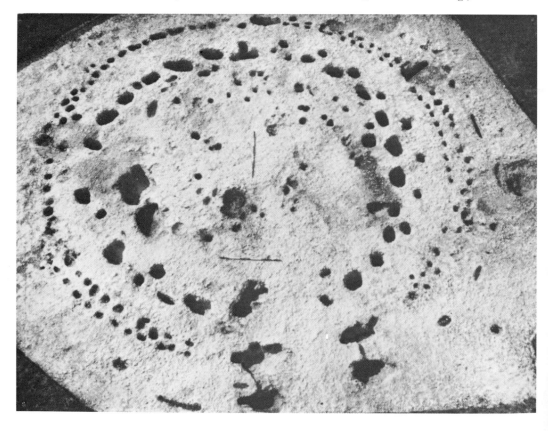

historical museum, showing not only representations, but those representations within the context of the changing seasons. After all, a farm is a living unit and the demonstration area had to be so too. Very quickly it was realised that the best, if not the only way, was to regard the new area as a research annexe to the Ancient Farm and to consider it as an integral part of the whole, and not as a separate entity.

Work began in mid-January 1976, once reluctant planners had finally given permission. To their credit, few planners can have been faced with similar applications involving the construction of strange earthworks and a Celtic manor house, field systems for the propagation of prehistoric cereals and paddocks to house rare animals.

The lay-out was designed to simulate as far as possible an enclosure of Iron-Age type surrounded by fields and paddocks. Public access was to be along the tracks between these features. With any museum, whether living historical or static historical, there needs to be a clear focal point which will serve as a pivot for the site and a major attraction to draw in the visitor. For our purposes this was to be the central enclosure containing the largest reconstruction of a prehistoric roundhouse ever undertaken anywhere. Timber had already been collected for this major experiment long before the chance to build a demonstration area had ever arisen. Experiment, if not risk, permeated the planning, as there seemed little point in repeating what had already been done on the Ancient Farm itself.

Since the house itself was an experiment, all the stages of the experimental formula had to be experienced. The basic archaeological data were drawn from an excavation at Pimperne in Dorset where the evidence of a large roundhouse had been recovered. In fact, the remains of two successive houses were discovered on a site thought to have been continuously occupied for about four hundred years. The building we were contemplating was not an ephemeral structure of a decade or so but one capable of standing for many generations. The excavation plans and the extraction can be seen in figs. 3a, b. The evidence suggests a structure some 12.8 metres in diameter comprising an outer stake wall, an inner ring of free-standing posts, a massive entrance porch with two small doors on either side and a further door slightly offset from the diameter at the rear of the building. The interpretation of the evidence as a house depends largely upon the presence of the hearth and the spread of pot sherds which would be unlikely to be present in a barn.

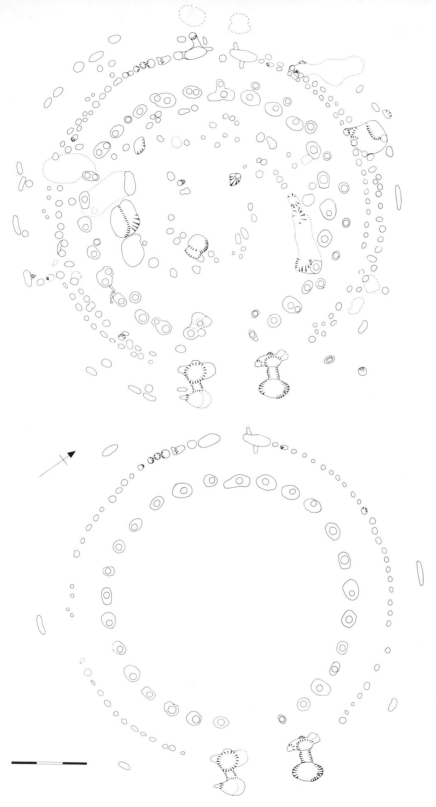

The plan as drawn in fig. 3b is the usual system adopted for the presentation of such archaeological data. Even with the scale it hardly conveys a real appreciation of size. It is quite remarkable how even the excavation area itself fails to impress in readily comprehensible terms. It is only when one begins to enclose physically the space in question that the enormousness of the structure is finally realised. As with previous reconstructions, the ground evidence was rigidly followed. The outer wall of stakes was first constructed and the principle of the ring, so important to withstand the roof pressure on a round-house, was followed by firmly jointing the outer wall into the porch timbers. Hazel rods were interwoven between the stakes. The inner ring of posts, each one free-standing, was surmounted by a continuous lintel some three metres above the ground. Joinery was modelled on neolithic and Bronze-Age evidence of mortice and tenon joints, scarf joints and wooden pegs. The inner ring is remarkably reminiscent of Stonehenge and is readily recognised as a copy.

The raising of the first rafter not only represented a considerable feat of strength on the part of the two builders

OPPOSITE
Fig. 3a The excavation plan of the Pimperne site, showing traces of two houses.

Fig. 3b The ground plan of the reconstructed Pimperne house extracted from the excavation plan.

The Pimperne house: this stage of the construction shows all the upright timbers in place as evidenced by the archaeological excavation.

but also a justification of the experiment as a whole. In fact, the rafter toppled over the inner ring almost destroying half of the work force. In order for the rafter to reach the central point of the roof at a pitch of 45°, it had to be over 11 metres long. The weight distribution of such a length of timber was disproportionate, much the heavier section being above the ring. However, by placing the butt end on the ground a point of balance was restored and stability achieved. This solution was supported by the evidence from the archaeological ground plan. Around the perimeter of the house on the plan are six shallow, elongated scoops, previously thought to indicate a possible third wall. They represent the ideal resting place for the butt ends of the major rafters. Further they indicate that there were six of these.

Using this evidence, six elm rafters were duly positioned, and it was quickly realised that towards the apex of the roof the distance between these major rafters was ideal for the positioning of a horizontal ring, previously found to be vital, which would support the remaining rafters without distorting the conical shape of the roof. Also the position of the ring occurred one third down the slant length of the rafters at the

The Pimperne house: the main rafters and ring beam in place.

critical point of stress. At the time the logic was irrefutable and subsequently has remained so. Ultimately these main rafter butts will be sawn off to correspond with the others allowing an eave of just 0.6 metres. Finally, the elongated shape of the scoop was explained because it allowed adjustments to be made for the main rafters. A small movement at ground level was a considerable one some six metres in the air. Thus one can probably distinguish, certainly in this case, between structural and constructional features.

The remaining rafters, each one jointed onto the outer wall, make up the full apex of the roof. It is well worth recording that all this work was achieved by just two people although the ideal construction force would be three. The physical execution of such a structure lends some possible insight into prehistoric construction techniques, and belies the old saw that many hands make light work. More than three people working on this house would have been a positive hindrance to progress.

The final phases of construction were similar to those described in an earlier chapter. The purlins, split hazel rods, were lashed into prepared notches on the rafters at twenty-five centimetre intervals, to provide a support and anchorage for

The Pimperne house: rafters and ring beam form an intricate pattern in the apex of the roof.

the thatch. The porch presented few problems beyond the massive nature of the timbers. The lintels alone weigh in excess of 150 kg. The infill to the porch sides follows the same principles of interweaving, but this time within the braced framework.

Technical details both of the materials and the construction of this house are interesting from a number of different standpoints. The stake-holes in the outer-ring are no more than 15 cm deep, and the major post-holes rarely exceed 45 cm. The diameter of the house is 12.8 m and from ground to apex 8 m. Each rafter weighs on average approximately 150 kg. Over two hundred trees were used in the reconstruction. All the upright timbers were oak, the six major rafters were elm and the rest were ash. Interweaving the walls and the side panels of the porch used the rods from over eighty good coppiced hazel stools. The roof weight when dry exceeds ten tonnes.

The most obvious implications of these details is the timber required for the structure. Fifty straight oak trees, coppice grown and averaging forty years old, were used in the structure. Straight ash and elm trees nine metres and more in length were used for rafters. Such oak and ash trees can only be obtained from carefully managed and controlled woodland. Incidentally, the spreading oak traditionally associated with the village green and local cricket matches is a very poor relation of the majestic, straight, tight-grained oak required by the prehistoric and medieval house builder, as well as the ship builder of more recent times. It is the age at which timber becomes useful which perhaps is the key. From sapling to maturity spans a human generation. Can we see a forward planning policy of one generation being concerned with supplies for the next? Hazel and most probably willow were coppiced from the neolithic period, and even here the rotation involves a span of seven to ten years. The need for timber, indeed, suggests a complex and settled service industry. At this time in prehistory it could sensibly be argued that it was also a traditional industry.

The thatch for the roof, in this case four tonnes of wheat straw, but it could have been river reed, represents the product from at least 1.6 hectares of arable land, that is, between fifteen and twenty Celtic fields. The six weeks required to put it on, a conservative time estimate agreed by several professional thatchers, argues, again, for at least the presence of a jobbing thatcher. Few farmers, and certainly not the farmers from a labour-intensive system, can afford six weeks out of the season to thatch a house. This is yet another instance where a service industry probably existed.

The builders themselves are most unlikely to have been anything other than professional. Potentially, we can even envisage both a timber yard and a builders' yard. The joinery is constructed as the building evolves, and one suspects that the positioning of post-holes is directed not by symmetry but by expediency. The plans appear to be regular, but in reality are far removed from it. Consequently, principles of pre-fabrication must be discounted. Also we must ignore the parallels offered by African practices. Their houses share only the circular plan and cone-shaped roof, thereafter all comparisons founder. The life expectancy of an average African house is optimistically five years. In the British climate perhaps two years would be a generous estimate for such houses. Recent experiments in Denmark suggest an even shorter period. The African house, wholly successful for its purpose, is built within the context of a hostile environment. Standing timbers and roof coverings and ties are destroyed extremely rapidly by the voracious insect population. Accordingly, building systems are rough and ready in the full knowledge that all will have to be done again within the relatively near future. Indeed, it is not uncommon for the prospective African house-builder to start preparing for his next dwelling by brewing up many gallons of beer, the incentive for his friends to help him in the construction.

This particular reconstruction of the Pimperne house makes a major contribution to our understanding of the physical scale of prehistoric houses. Even if all the timber is wrongly jointed together and the straw is thatched on in an unlikely way, the space enclosed by the structure is most likely to be correct. The materials of the construction are as accurate as can be assumed from both archaeological and documentary sources. Consequently, the space itself, the volume and atmosphere of the house can be studied. It is noteworthy that a modern house with every convenience could be placed within this structure.

Finally, because the house now exists, attention can be focused upon the most tantalising question of all, how this house in particular and other houses in general were actually used in the Iron Age. Remarkably, there is almost no clear evidence of function yet recorded. This may be due to the manner of modern excavation and the ubiquitous use of earthmoving machines or, more unlikely, because this evidence no longer exists. Was a house like the Pimperne house

a Celtic manor? Can we envisage the occupant as the local
aristocrat or was he the middle-man of the successful agricultural economy? Is this house a place of feasting – an activity
to which, according to the Romans, the Celts were addicted –
or is it a place of politics or both?

The livestock and crop husbandry elements of the demonstration area have all been discussed elsewhere in this volume.
The remaining feature is the experimental earthwork which

The completed Pimperne house: the focal point of the Demonstration Area, this structure is the largest reconstruction of a prehistoric round-house ever undertaken anywhere.

encloses the Pimperne House and completes the focal unit. The conflict between demonstration and experiment was again settled in favour of the latter. The simple philosophy adopted is that an experiment, if a little more difficult to understand, is ultimately much more appreciated by the layman because there is no question of offering any kind of sop to his intelligence.

From the middle and late Bronze Age farmsteads were

Firedogs and oven. The interior of the Pimperne house dressed for a scene in a film.

commonly enclosed by a simple ditch and bank, a practice which continued throughout the Iron Age, with increasing complexity in their layout and planning. As field remains these usually consist of a low earthen bank with a parallel shallow depression. Fifty years ago many of these field remains were visible to the naked eye, but with the increase in ploughing and the advent of deeper and heavier ploughs these remains have largely been ploughed out, and their location is only made possible by aerial photography.

The ditches, often now without any accompanying bank, vary considerably in size and shape. Similarly, the plans they follow are also extremely variable although it is possible to suggest loose categories. Excavation reveals their profile or section and occasionally it is possible to ascribe a date from artefactual evidence. More interesting from the practical point of view is the method of their construction and thereafter their steady deterioration.

Much attention is paid to silting patterns, especially the very earliest layers at the bottom of the ditch, because from these layers, quickly sealed by subsequent silting, it is occasionally possible to discover micro-faunal and pollen evidence which may allow some explanation of the adjacent land area. Because of the importance of such excavation for interpretation, it has been the subject of a major experimental programme involving the construction of two earthworks on different soil types at Overton Down and Wareham Down respectively. This programme has been deliberately restricted to the examination of a linear straight-sided flat-bottom ditch with a parallel earth mound constructed of the excavated material. At Butser and earlier at Avoncroft Museum in Worcestershire further earthwork experiments have been constructed by the author.

These experiments were designed specifically to replicate a typical Iron-Age type ditch and bank and to observe the deterioration process over a period of time. Since experiment in this area is, at this stage, a learning process, it is only accurate to describe both of these experimental earthworks as pilot schemes leading to a fully controlled and monitored programme.

As a broad generalisation the typical ditch confining an Iron Age settlement is 'V' shaped in section and averages 1.50 m deep and 1.50 m across the top. It must be emphasised that

The ditch and bank in the Demonstration Area is an experimental earthwork. The erosion from the sides of the ditches is being carefully monitored.

these are average figures although, contrary to statistics where the average does not necessarily exist, ditches of these dimensions are not uncommon. The first ditch and bank was constructed in the autumn of 1969 at Avoncroft Museum. There two lengths of ditch to the above dimensions were dug by hand, the upcast material forming a simple dump bank without any berm or gap between the edge of the ditch and the bank. The soil type was marl. Vertical measuring rods graduated in centimetres were set in the bottom of the ditch. Both lengths were further fenced off from human and animal interference. During the first winter both ditches were flooded to a depth of 1.20 m. After six months and the subsidence of the flood water one centimetre of silt was recorded. Three months later a further half centimetre was recorded and thereafter both ditch and bank were covered in luxuriant vegetation. This had the effect of stabilising both of them and despite annual winter flooding no further silt deposits were recorded until the end of the experiment in 1973. Clearly in this soil type there would be little joy for the archaeologist.

The demonstration area of the Ancient Farm afforded the opportunity of carrying this experiment further, albeit on the different and perhaps more suitable soil type of chalk. Excavation on marl, for example, is fiendishly difficult since disturbed and non-disturbed soil and subsoil hold together in an almost indistinguishable way. The earthwork at Butser was modelled in terms of its general plan on an Iron Age site at East Castle, Steeple Langford in Dorset. The ditch, of the same dimensions as above, was excavated by a machine utilising a small triangular-shaped bucket with a capacity equivalent to four shovels. This allowed minimal compaction of the upcast material. One major change in design was introduced with the inclusion of a narrow berm some 30 cm wide. The turf from the ditch surface was built into low retaining walls no more than 30 cm high on either side of the bank. The upcast material from the ditch was piled between these walls and roughly shaped down with a shovel. Finally after four weeks, in which time the material settled, a palisade fence was erected on top of the bank. The end product is visually what we imagine a typical Iron Age ditch and bank to have been and thus the purpose of demonstration is fulfilled. Archaeologically the experiment has barely begun. The first year of its life is, in many ways, the most important from the point of view of the primary silt and micro-faunal and pollen remains. The work was completed in April 1976, since experience from the Avoncroft earthwork argued for an earlier construction date than the autumn.

During the summer of 1976, the year of the great drought, the earthwork more than fulfilled its demonstration role. The chalk was a resplendent white and the ditch clear cut and immaculate. The signal observation was the vegetation activity on the narrow berm. The grass flourished and achieved a strong verdant growth, entirely contrary to the surrounding area. It also provided a living barrier which prevented any fall or slip of material from the bank into the ditch bottom. The winter came and with it the inevitable rain storms (the winter of 1976–77 was one of the wettest on record) and frost. At last things began to happen. Erosion initially came from the topsoil cover, earth slipping down from the exposed face of the soil. During the frosts the chalk sides began to fragment slightly and tiny pieces with the occasional larger blocks trickled into the ditch bottom gradually covering the initial soil slip. The vegetation barrier prevented any bank material from entering the ditch. Thus after one year the data return is extremely significant. Two layers of silt material, neither of which come from the bank, form the lowest layers in the ditch.

In terms of interpretation we have a fundamentally new approach to ditch-silting patterns; it clearly requires further experimental work, but nonetheless the implications are

Students learning the rudiments of making pottery. Courses in various aspects of archaeology are regularly held at the Ancient Farm.

obvious. The first layer of silt comes from the original ground surface within a few months of construction. The micro evidence, therefore, will reflect the immediate landscape at that time. This is critical since the original land surface has often been destroyed by subsequent activity. This layer is sealed by material from the ditch sides and it is possible to consider frost intensity from granule size, the more intense the frost, the more the rock is broken down. Projecting forward, as the ditch sides erode away reaching an angle of rest, the berm will disappear and finally silting will occur from the bank itself. This third layer may well contain micro-evidence which will reflect the nature of the landscape during the period of settlement. There is, of course, a great deal more to be learned from this kind of experiment, but at present the first results require a general reappraisal of ditch sections and their source. There is no doubt that this approach by experiment is the key to the future.

The demonstration area was constructed to show to all sectors of the public the elements of the research which is in process at the Ancient Farm itself. It is extremely important

H.M. The Queen visited the Demonstration Area of the Ancient Farm in August 1976.

that any research programme fulfils its educational obligations and responsibilities. To be able to achieve that end by creating an annexe to a research area is perhaps the happiest of all solutions. Already many thousands of schoolchildren have visited the demonstration area in organised parties. A large number of schools use it as a major resource, and at last prehistory in general and the Iron Age in particular are finding their rightful places in school curricula. Students, both undergraduate and graduate, avail themselves of the opportunity to study within the confines of this unique project. Finally, the public are able to see and appreciate at first hand the problems posed by prehistory and the practical solutions offered.

Perhaps the most mundane and yet the most important motivation for the construction of this demonstration area is the need for financial support for the project as a whole. Research of this nature is necessarily long-term and cannot successfully be viewed in three-year periods. For example, it will be twenty years before statistically valid results will be in hand from the crop experiments alone. Thus the demonstration area, should it succeed in its intention to show to the people in the most exciting way yet attempted a complex and involved research project, by their interest and support will achieve financial stability. Today it is a pioneer project, struggling even to survive. Tomorrow its contribution to prehistory may well be incalculable.

Index